From A Different Perspective

Heather Thorne

Self published by Heather Thorne in 2024 through *We Inspire Now Books*, a business assisting authors to self-publish.

Copyright © 2024 Heather Thorne

ISBNs
Print: 978-0-6453052-7-2
Ebook   978-0-6458252-6-8

Heather Thorne has asserted her right under the Copyright Act 1968 to be identified as the author of this work. The information in this book is based on the author's experiences and opinions.

The author takes responsibility for the content and for any permissions to use information. Any breaches will be rectified in further editions of the book.

This work is copyright. Apart from any use permitted under the Copyright Act 1968, no part of this publication may be reproduced, stored in or introduced into a retrieval system, or transmitted in any form, or by any means (electronic, mechanical, photocopying, recording or otherwise) without the prior written permission of the author. Any person who commits any unauthorised act in relation to this publication may be liable to criminal prosecution and civil claims for damages. Enquiries should be made through *We Inspire Now Books*.

Cover Image:	Original image sourced from the website: www.unsplash.com annie-spratt-dyMun0gD6hk-unsplash
Cover Design:	We Inspire Now Books
Layout:	Antoinette Pellegrini We Inspire Now Books

We Inspire Now Books
PO BOX 133 Greensborough,
Victoria Australia 3088
www.weinspirenowbooks.com

Dedication

This book is dedicated to my younger self, who didn't know who she really was.

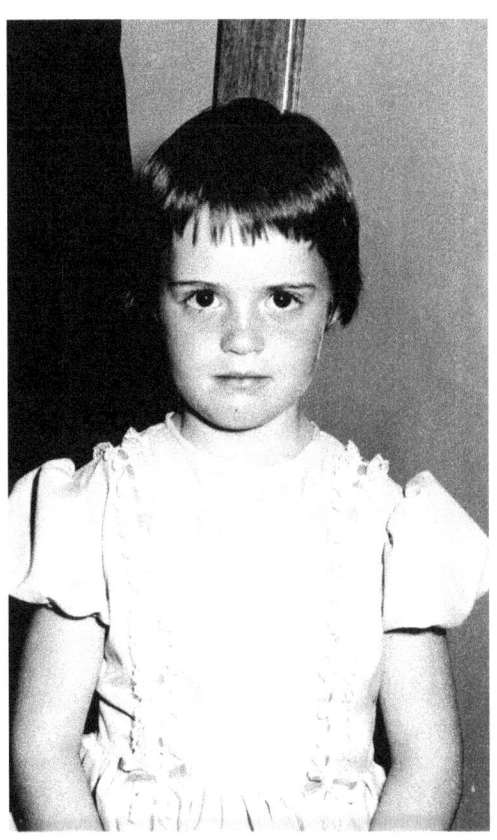

Contents

Note To The Reader		1
Chapter 1:	My Adventure	7
Chapter 2	The Early Years	13
Chapter 3:	Life Changes Forever	23
Chapter 4:	Independent Career Woman	37
Chapter 5:	Married Life	47
Chapter 6:	The Sandwich Generation	61
Chapter 7:	The Awakening Begins	69
Chapter 8:	The Family Secret	79
Chapter 9:	Endings and New Beginnings	85
Chapter 10:	Becoming Me	93
Chapter 11:	A Life-Long Learner	103
Author Bio		111
Appendix	Information on Energy Profiling by Carol Tuttle	113

A Note To The Reader

Dear Reader,

Until 2021, when I contributed a story to an anthology called *Journey to Me*[1], I had no thoughts about writing a book or any ambitions to be an author. Once I decided to write this book, the words have filled the pages of my notebook, and I've thoroughly enjoyed the writing process. It has been healing, too.

I have found my voice, and I'm using it to inspire, motivate and educate women over 50, in particular.

---

[1] Antoinette Pellegrini, *Journey To Me: A Discovery of Self*, Book 3 We Inspire Now Anthology Series, We Inspire Now Books, Victoria, 2021

Fifty was a watershed age for me. What worked before that age didn't work any more. My mind was being opened by university study, and I was making new friends. My marriage was slowly coming to an end, and I felt very lonely in it.

My *real-life* education didn't start until 2018, when I first started studying Bob Proctor's materials. Until then, I had no idea how the mind works, what a paradigm is and how to change it. I was sleep-walking through life to a large degree. It was in that first course that I came across this definition of education. It has been attributed to both Abraham Lincoln and John Ruskin, a nineteenth-century British educator.

'Education does not mean teaching people what they do not know. It means teaching them to behave as they do not behave.'

This quote resonated with me the first time I heard it at the age of 57. I had not heard about it at teachers' college in my twenties. Nor did it come up in my Bachelor of Education course or my Health Promotion degree two decades later. I was stunned that, as a qualified and experienced teacher, I didn't know how the mind worked.

Writing this book has been a process of self-discovery and reflection. It has taken longer than I had anticipated because I have found professionals who have added immensely to my understanding. One of these is Dr Gabor Maté, who has written about the health consequences of childhood trauma.

A Note To The Reader

You will relate to some of the experiences I share more easily than others. I appreciate that my perspective is that of a western, heterosexual woman, who has lived her entire life in a first-world country. I can't change where I was born or raised, but I can choose to be open-minded and inclusive of people with different experiences and perspectives.

I firmly believe that this book is in your hands on purpose. It may have been a gift, or you may have bought it or borrowed it from the library. Whichever way you came to have it, it's meant for you. How do I know this? Many years ago, I came across my favourite book, *Conversations with God*[2] by Neale Donald Walsch, in a library. I was in a hurry, and the book was on a trolley when it caught my eye. It was as if it was saying, 'pick me'. I'm so glad I did. Have you ever had a book practically jump off the shelf into your hands?

It is entirely your choice, as a thinking person, to accept or reject the ideas expressed in the following pages. However, I hope you find yourself nodding in agreement as you read. I hope you say, 'That's interesting' now and again.

Sixty was a watershed age for me. I said the same about 50, but this was different. For a start, Australia was in the first year of the COVID-19 pandemic. For me, turning 60 made me realise that I do have a voice, and I've decided to use it. I want to share the wisdom and experience I have gained over the past decades. If

---

[2] Neale Donald Walsch, *Conversations with God: An Uncommon Dialogue*, Book 1, Sydney, Hodder, 1996

it were possible to go back in time and be 30 years old again, I would only do it if I could take my 60-year-old head with me. People laugh when I say this, but I really don't want to go back to my younger years and do it all again.

I like where I am in my life. Now that my daughters are independent young women, leading their own lives very capably, I am free to pursue my interests and goals. With my wonderful, loving partner, I'm focused on living life to the fullest and making beautiful memories.

Living through the pandemic in the city with the unenviable distinction of being the most locked-down city in the world taught me to appreciate today. Before the pandemic, when life appeared more predictable, I was taking time for granted. Predictably, it is an illusion. Change is the only certainty in this life. I embrace change, but sometimes, the pace can be exhausting.

Now, I have a greater appreciation for the simple things in life, and I keep a daily gratitude journal. I am aware that I can't know what's around the next corner, and I don't know how much time I have left: no-one does. That is why this saying has always been special to me:

'Yesterday is history. Tomorrow is a mystery. Today is a gift, and that's why it's called the present.' (Anonymous)

A Note To The Reader

I hope that by the time you come to the end of this book, you'll realise that it's never too late to change the way you think about yourself. I have a much different, more expansive view of myself as a result of my personal development journey of the last five years. Limited views of myself and my potential have been gradually replaced, and the process is ongoing.

I have a big-picture view of my life and can see pivotal events have shaped the woman I am today. The process of examining my upbringing in detail has revealed the way I was conditioned to think and behave. Therefore, I encourage you to take a close look at the ways in which you were programmed. Some of your habits may no longer serve you, if they ever did. It takes courage, but it can be really worthwhile. Take it from me.

Chapter 1
My Adventure

From A Different Perspective

The events of April 26, 2018 are indelibly imprinted on my mind, just like the birth of each of my daughters. It was the day I left Perth to start a new life in Melbourne. It was the beginning of my adventure.

I left Perth with two suitcases on a one-way flight to Melbourne. It wasn't that I didn't like living in Perth, but I was yearning for a new life in a bigger city. Perth was all I had known. Since 2012, when my younger daughter left home to study at the University of Melbourne, I had visited once or twice a year. In 2016, I decided that I would relocate, but I had to wait until the time was right.

In 2016, my mother was still alive and had been living in a nursing home for ten years. She had advanced Alzheimer's disease, was bedbound, and non-verbal. I took turns with my sister, visiting Mum several times a week. While Mum was alive, Perth was where I was needed and wanted to be.

My life was hectic at that time. I was finishing my final semester of a Bachelor of Health Promotion degree at the University of Notre Dame, studying part-time. It eventually took me seven years to complete, as my marriage broke up at the end of my second year. It was too hard to study with all the emotional turmoil I was experiencing, although I tried. My part-time job was not fulfilling me, but I didn't have the time or energy to look for anything else. Besides, what was the point if I was going to Melbourne?

Fast forward to 2018, and the time was finally right to embark on my adventure. Mum was no longer alive, and my sister and I had done all the 'firsts' – her birthday, our birthdays, Christmas etc. In January, my friend Barbara died from terminal liver disease. She was not quite 65, and the last year of her life had been very difficult. Witnessing her suffering wasn't easy at all. I made a promise to myself that when I was at the end of my life, I would have no regrets. I would not say, 'I was going to move to Melbourne, but I never did.'

My motto became, 'life if too short for this shit!' With that attitude, I resigned from my job. Just four weeks later, I was on a Qantas flight to Melbourne, buoyed by incredible excitement. I was making this dream a reality. As I flew from Perth to Melbourne that morning, I had no idea how much my life was about to change. Friends and former colleagues had told me I was brave, but I didn't see myself that way.

I felt like I had come to a different country; such was the extent of the difference between Melbourne and Perth. The biggest difference wasn't just the size of the city or the famed 'four seasons in one day' weather; it was the pace of life. I hit the ground running, in my usual style, and found a place to live. It wasn't until I was living in my new home that I realised the enormity of what I had done. Now that I had time to reflect, I came to appreciate how brave I was.

As I write this, four and a half years after the fact, I see that the real adventure was the personal growth journey I've undertaken. I could not have achieved that in Perth: I was too comfortable. I had to leave my home state, and all that was familiar there to find the real me. Up until then, I didn't know who I was. I just knew my roles – daughter, wife, mother, teacher, student, etc.

The best decision I made once in Melbourne was to join the Bob Proctor Coaching program (I'll refer to it as BPC from now on). Although I had read numerous self-help books as an adult, none of them impacted me the way that course did, and I know why. I would read the book and think that I knew the information it contained on an intellectual level. To really know it, I had to put it into practice, and change my behaviour.

For the first time, I understood how the mind works. I am still amazed that it took 57 years to get this information. In all my formal education, I was never given an explanation of the mind, and I am a teacher!

I don't usually write poetry, but one day, I felt drawn to express myself in verse:

The woman I am now

The woman I am now
In my seventh decade of life
Is a world away from who she was
Even a few years ago.
That's a good thing.
If given the chance,
by a genie or a fairy godmother perhaps,
to be thirty again
I would say, 'No way!'
'Not unless I could take my 60-year-old head with me'.
I would not forgo all the growth I have achieved.
I would not leave behind all the wisdom gained through experience.
Those are priceless gifts.
The woman I am today is assertive and decisive.
I know what I want.
I know I can have it and
I am making it happen!

I wouldn't have been able to write something like that poem in my early adulthood. My roles defined me: daughter, student, and teacher. That was a very limited way of seeing myself. I can see that now. In the following pages, I delve into my childhood and adult experiences and reflect on them from a new perspective.

Chapter 2

The Early Years

I was born in 1960, part of the "Baby Boomer" generation, in Western Australia. It's been a long time since I was a child, but what I experienced had life-long repercussions for my health and happiness. Some memories, both happy and sad, are still vivid.

As a young adult, I believed I had had a happy childhood. I have changed my mind about that in the process of writing this book. There was stress and sadness in the household that I didn't consciously understand, but I picked up on subconsciously. As a baby and young child, I couldn't help picking up on what was going on around me. I understand that now, but my parents didn't when I was a baby.

My parents were both in their early 30s when I was born. Mum had been a teacher and was then a full-time housewife. In the late 1950s, women were not allowed to teach with the Education Department in WA if they were married. So, she was forced to resign when she married. My father was an accountant in a printing company. I have memories of going with him on the weekend to the office in Fremantle, playing with the rubber stamps while the printing machines worked noisily in the basement.

Sadly, I don't know a lot about my father's life before he met and married Mum. The little I do know was told to me by friends of the family and Mum. Born in 1928, the eldest of two boys, he grew up around Fremantle. According to a family friend who had known him at school, my father was painfully shy. The one story I heard many times, although not from Dad himself, was that his dream was to raise Hereford cattle in the South West of WA. However, that wasn't good enough for his mother, so he trained as an accountant after leaving school and joined a printing firm.

Dad was not physically robust, according to what I was told. His mother, maybe a hypochondriac herself, used to send her son to school with Bex headache tablets. That was 'just in case' he got a headache at school. The tablets eventually ruined his kidneys.

Another thing I learnt about Dad was that he was a worrier, not the ideal disposition for an accountant. Many years after his death, while clearing out the family home, my sister and I found one of Dad's school reports. We were surprised to see that English, not Maths, was his strength. Maybe he found accounting difficult for that reason.

I always felt sad for him, that he didn't have the chance to live the life he really wanted. The closest he ever came to having Hereford cattle was a ceramic ornament. The closest he came to having a farm was a citrus orchard that he partly owned. It was one of the reasons I believe that he succumbed to depression. He was living the life that his mother and society expected him to, but it didn't make him happy.

Although I will never know the whole story because my parents have both died, I believe that the stress in my early life was caused by my father's depression. It wasn't his fault, and there's no blame. At the time, children were not told about adult issues, and mental illness was a taboo subject. That didn't mean it didn't impact me.

Although it was not discovered until I was six months old, I was born with an underactive thyroid. There was no heel prick test then. Hypothyroidism is one of the conditions newborn babies are now screened for. Fortunately, I was diagnosed and treated before I became mentally retarded, one of the consequences of hypothyroidism. I was started on artificial thyroxine, which I would have to take for life.

Growing up, I was continually told that I was clumsy and unco-ordinated because of my underactive thyroid. I believed what I was told, so I didn't try to do things like somersaults and cartwheels. It stopped me from climbing and swinging at the playground like my sister. My parents never gave me a bike, so I never learnt to ride one. They were scared I would fall off and hurt myself.

What really limited me was the belief that I had taken on about myself. I understand that my parents were just trying to protect me from harm. However, it harmed my self-esteem and self-image while keeping my body safe. That turned out to be a more serious injury than any I may have sustained by falling off a bike. Broken bones heal quicker than damaged self-esteem.

In the 1960s, parents were in charge of the family. My younger sister and I were raised to be well-behaved and respectful. Family life was ordered and predictable. We knew our roles. Our evening meal was eaten at the dining table, and we had our designated seats. The TV was never on, and putting your elbows on the table was a definite no-no. We had to wait for permission to leave the table when the meal was over.

As the older child, I learnt that I had to be a 'good girl'. That meant I sometimes had to suppress my natural tendencies to move quickly, act impetuously and talk excitedly. I was told to, 'settle down' and 'calm down'. My exuberance was too much for my parents, particularly my father. I understood that I had to be quiet when Dad wasn't feeling well.

My earliest memory clearly demonstrated my true extroverted nature. It was my sister's first birthday, and I was nearly three years old. Mum had made and decorated a cake which was on the tray of the high chair. I clearly remember thinking to myself, 'This is a boring photo. It needs some action.' Just as Mum was about to take the photo, I grabbed a handful of cake in one hand and a hunk of my sister's hair in the other. I wanted it to look like she was eating the cake. She burst into tears. Mum and my grandmothers 'told me off'. I was only a little girl who was being herself.

Instead, I was shamed for my spontaneity. That was a wound that I subconsciously carried with me for many years. I never did it again and curbed my exuberance in case it got me into trouble. The lesson I learnt from incidents like the one just described was that it wasn't safe to be my natural self.

As a young child, I suffered a lot from tonsillitis but never had my tonsils removed. I still remember our very stern doctor saying, 'If she gets it again, I'll take her tonsils out.' Strangely, I didn't get it again. It must have been frightened out of me.

Sometimes, there were unexpected perks from being sick. For example, one time, while Mum and I were waiting to see the doctor, she bought a raffle ticket for a Christmas stocking. She won it, and we girls were very excited. It was huge, probably about six feet, and full of all sorts of toys. My sister and I were allowed to pick one toy each, and the rest were donated to 'less fortunate' children.

My true nature was suppressed in order to fit in with my family, but it occasionally revealed itself. I couldn't always be a 'good girl'. One time, at the holiday house in Rockingham, Dad was looking after my sister and me while Mum had a rest. I wanted an icecream from the corner shop but Dad said 'No'. There was no fence around the house, and I was able to sneak away to the shop when Dad was distracted. At the shop, I bought an icecream, knowing that I didn't have any money to pay for it. The shop assistant wasn't happy so I had to leave it behind and go home and tell Dad.

The Early Years

Needless to say, I was 'growled at', and I didn't get the icecream.

I was a determined child. For example, I can still clearly remember when I was five, in year one at Primary School, and I wanted to go to school with just a tiny case and an apple. I'm not sure why I wanted to do that, but I suspect it was to regain some control in my life. I planned how I was going to do it and carried out my plan successfully by my standards.

My poor mother must have been frantic when she got up and discovered I was gone! She found me at school, which was about five minutes from home. It seemed to me that she arrived in her dark green Mini just after me. It probably seemed a long time to her. I honestly can't recall what happened as a result of my actions, but I know that I never repeated them. Looking back, it was an audacious act for a little girl, and even now, I am quite proud of my ability to pull it off.

It is hard to write about what our family life was like when I was a young child. All I have is vague impressions, a sense of what it was like. I felt the tension, saw the concern on my mother's face, the looks between adults that I glimpsed. In the 1960s, adults didn't realise I was picking up what wasn't said, reading between the lines, as it were.

The adults in our life did their best to protect me and my sister from what was going on. I remember one time when I was maybe five years old, Dad went away for a while. When he came back, I was very emotional, and tearful, and both my parents were surprised by my reaction. Another time, my parents suddenly left us with our grandparents for a short holiday in the country. It was strange because they didn't usually do things like that, and I don't remember them being very happy when they returned.

Dad, at times, was very quiet and didn't interact with us. He was emotionally unavailable. On those occasions, I had to be quiet, considerate, and move calmly for Dad's sake. I had to subdue my natural tendencies. That was the beginning of my conditioning, the roots of my belief that it was my job to put other people's emotional needs before mine, especially the needs of the men in my life. I learned that lesson well.

Another belief that I formed in childhood was that men in my life would suddenly disappear. The most important man at that time, my father, would disappear without warning. He didn't always say goodbye to me before he left or give me any idea when he would return. His absences were unpredictable and upsetting.

This story is a good example of these disappearances. One night, Dad was home with my sister and me while Mum went out by herself. I don't remember that happening very often, so it stands out in my mind. I woke up, and the house seemed very quiet. The TV wasn't on. Where was Dad? I got up and looked for him, but he wasn't in the house. I thought he might have gone next door, so I woke my sister, and we went to look for him. It was pitch black and scary.

We snuck up to the neighbours' back door but we couldn't hear or see Dad. So, worried and confused, we returned to our place, but he still wasn't home. When I woke the next morning, he was there. Phew! What a relief. I'm sure Dad had no idea how his actions affected his daughters. He probably thought we slept through his absence and were none the wiser.

Growing up, I didn't feel emotionally safe, at least some of the time. I didn't feel safe to express my feelings. My body has always responded to stress by putting on weight. The extra weight was a protection, at a subconscious level. By the time I was ten years old, I was already a big girl. I ate to comfort myself. I ate quickly, not tasting the food, just shovelling it in. I ate my feelings because I had no other strategies to deal with them.

At ten, while on holidays with my family in New Zealand, my periods started. That was another thing blamed on my underactive thyroid. It was more likely that my weight triggered the early onset of puberty as I already had breasts and had grown in height. I wasn't entirely uninformed as Mum had given me a booklet to read. It said that fourteen was the average age for the onset of periods, so I thought I had a while to go.

My physical childhood was over with the onset of my periods. On that holiday, I also started to show signs of anxiety. I developed a pain in one of my heels, like I had stepped on a bone, but there was nothing to see. I was reacting to the underlying tension in the family, even though we were on holiday.

That holiday to New Zealand was the last family holiday we took with Dad, as it turned out. It was a big adventure for my sister and me as we had never been on a plane before. We stayed with Mum's sister's family and travelled around the North Island by car. It was a very memorable holiday. Writing this, it occurred to me that it was probably the last time my aunt and her family saw Dad.

Chapter 3
Life Changes Forever

My life changed forever on Monday 29th November, 1971. I will never forget the events of that day; they are firmly imprinted on my memory. The emotional charge of the memories has been strong over the years, reinforced by reliving them.

My sister and I were getting ready for school. I was eleven, and she was nine. I had only turned eleven at the beginning of November and had a birthday party at home. Dad was there. I remember because he told me I couldn't wear my new watch to school and I was disappointed. He must have gone into hospital shortly after my party.

There was nothing to indicate that we would receive the most devastating news that morning. I don't even have to close my eyes to visualise us sitting at the table eating breakfast while Mum was at the kitchen sink. Suddenly, the doorbell rang. I instinctively jumped up to answer the door. There were two policemen who asked, 'Is your mother here?'

Instantly, clearly, I knew that Dad had died. I have no idea how I knew, but I did. I went to get Mum. When I returned to the kitchen table to resume breakfast, I knew I couldn't tell my sister. For a fleeting moment, I doubted myself, but I knew I was right. Mum came back into the house, absolutely distraught. My sister and I had never seen her so upset.

Our next-door neighbour arrived shortly afterwards. That wasn't unusual as she and Mum were friends, and her husband had died the year before. He and Dad had been best friends. I later learned that she had seen the police car arrive at our house as she was taking her daughter to school. Around the breakfast table, Mum told us that Dad had died in his sleep from a heart attack. We didn't question what she told us; she was our mother, and we trusted her. We didn't go to school that day.

My mother's sister came over from New Zealand, and plans were made for the funeral. My sister and I were not allowed to go to Dad's funeral; children didn't go to funerals in those days. It was even unusual for women to attend funerals. So, we didn't get the chance to say 'goodbye' in a ceremonial way, and that was regrettable.

We were allowed to attend the wake, however I have absolutely no recollection of the event. What I do remember was being told about my Dad's mother leaving the wake early to show off the renovations her surviving son had made to his house to relatives on his side of the family. That really hurt because it was disrespectful to Dad, Mum and us. I could not understand her behaviour at all, as a child.

After the funeral, the three of us had to continue living. I remember one afternoon, realising that Dad would never again come through the door at 5 pm, as was his habit. It just hit me. One day, Mum gave each of us a framed photo of Dad. That was all that we had besides our memories. We didn't talk about Dad at all. I think it was just too painful for all of us, so we avoided it.

There was no grief counselling in those days. The internet didn't exist, so Mum couldn't just Google how to guide us through the process. I don't even know if there was anything she could have read on the subject. So, we just got on with life the best we could. We kept busy. That was our default mechanism. Somehow, we were able to put one foot in front of another, but at times, it must have felt like wading through mud.

Did the trauma make all of us more resilient? Or were we already resilient, and that enabled us to cope with the trauma? It was probably a bit of both, I think. Mum, my sister, and I prided ourselves on being able to get on with our lives despite the loss of the main breadwinner. Maybe, each of us thought we had to suppress our emotions so that the others wouldn't be upset.

Reflecting on this period in my life from a distance of five decades, I can clearly see that I felt victimised by the events in my life over which I had had no control. It was a traumatic time in the lives of my mother, sister and myself, without a doubt. However, after the personal development work I've undertaken over the last few years, I've been able to change my perspective. I've learnt that when you change your perspective about anything, the thing itself changes.

There was a lot of loss in my life as a teenager. After the death of our father, my sister and I were also abandoned by his mother and brother. Inexplicably, our grandmother openly showed favouritism for our cousins by visiting them and not us. We could see her get off the bus right outside our house, walk around the corner and up the driveway to their place. It was right over the road. On my thirteenth birthday, I asked my grandmother why she hadn't visited me. That was a rare act of assertiveness on my part, but I was sufficiently hurt to confront her. Her reply did nothing to make me feel better about myself; I had come in second to a garden incinerator.

My sister and I didn't see my grandmother after that incident. It was the final straw for our mother, who had seen the harm done to her daughters over about two years after Dad's death. So, she confronted her Mother-in-Law and asked her to stop, or she would lose contact with us. She didn't stop her behaviour because she didn't think Mum would ban her from our lives. She thought wrong.

I admire Mum for taking that action. In doing so, she not only ended the emotional abuse our grandmother was meting out, but she set an excellent example for me. Be assertive with a person whose behaviour is toxic. If they continue, cut ties and don't look back. In our case, blood was not thicker than water.

Fortunately, Mum's mother was a completely different person; kind, gentle and loving. She was very dear to us, and we spent a lot of time with her. One of my enduring memories of her was when she celebrated her 50th wedding anniversary on the same day that I turned ten, the 4th of November 1970. It was a very special occasion, and the family took my grandparents to lunch at the Palace Restaurant in Perth city. It was the full works; silver service and lots of cutlery. Mum and Dad had taught my sister and me how to behave in that setting, and we were on our best behaviour.

As a child, Nana, Mum's mother, had suffered from Rheumatic Fever, which had weakened her heart. Notwithstanding, she lived until 79, which was a major feat. The house my grandparents lived in was not at all age-friendly; it didn't even have an inside toilet. The washing was still done in a copper – a big copper bowl set into a concrete stand. A fire at the base heated the water, and clothes had to be lowered into the boiling water with a pair of wooden tongs, then hauled out again. Then the excess water was wrung out by putting the clothes through a manual wringer. It wasn't as if automatic washing machines didn't exist in the early 1970s; they just didn't have one.

Our already small family got even smaller in 1973 when we lost Nana to heart disease. At the time of her death, my sister and I had no inkling of the next big change in our lives. My grandfather, then 80 years old, came to live with Mum and us girls. At first, we were excited to have him move in. However, once the novelty wore off, we found that our lives revolved around the needs of an old man.

Grandpa had a number of chronic health conditions that impacted his lifestyle. One of those was Paget's disease, which caused his jaw bones to change shape. This in turn, meant his dentures didn't fit comfortably, and he couldn't eat hard food. I vividly remember one time when he bought a large box of fish directly from the boat. Grandpa loved fish and would happily have eaten it for breakfast, lunch and dinner. On the other hand, as a teenager, I got pretty sick of it.

Over time, it seemed that more and more compromises were required from my sister and me to fit in with our elderly grandfather. He was rigid in his way of thinking and doing things. For example, after dinner, Grandpa would wash the dishes, and we would wipe them. Grandpa's idea of washing up was to put everything in the sink at once and stir. If we noticed some dirt on an item and pointed it out to him, we were told, 'You haven't wiped it hard enough!' No way would he re-wash it. Mum eventually bought a dishwasher.

At the time, I put Grandpa's obstinacy down to his age. However, as I reflect on his behaviour from my present understanding, I believe there were other reasons for it. As I've already mentioned, he was a marine engineer, so he thought like an engineer. He may have had Asperger's syndrome, but nothing was known about that in the 1970s. In addition, he was used to being the authority figure in his household.

His wife and two daughters had given in to his way of doing things. It became their habit and mine as well.

One good example of this was when Mum and Dad built a duplex on the back of their property, specifically for Nana and Grandpa. Mum was both very disappointed and frustrated that, when the new home was finished, Grandpa refused to move. He wouldn't leave his shed! Mum knew that her mother would have loved a modern home with an inside toilet and a modern laundry. However, Grandpa dug his heels in, and they stayed where they were.

The experience of living with my grandfather as a teenager was crucial for me. I formed deep beliefs about my role as a woman. Without realising it consciously, I believed that it was my role to keep a man content, and the best way to do that was to give in, not argue, to push my needs down. I used to tell myself that, 'In the greater scheme of things, it doesn't matter'. That was rationalising, telling myself lies, because all the little things added up. At times, I felt very resentful, but I had nowhere to put those feelings. I ate them instead.

As a young teenager, for the first few years of high school, I was overweight. At the beginning of 1975, I embarked on a weight loss journey that was successful but very tough. In about ten months, I lost 16 kgs by sheer willpower. I was so hard on myself and, consequently, everyone else. For example, on Easter that year, Mum gave me raw cashews instead of chocolate. I prided myself on eating *one* cashew nut a day. That's how disciplined I was, and I was proud of it. Looking back, it was not a healthy approach to losing weight by any stretch of the imagination. Subconsciously, I didn't believe I had control of anything else in my life except what I put in my mouth.

According to what Mum told me later, I had taken my weight loss efforts too far and was even scared to drink water. I believed, mistakenly, that it had calories in it. Mum was a wise and caring woman and she must have been scared by what she saw me doing to myself. She persuaded me to abandon my efforts to lose more weight. I was thin enough. Thank Goodness I listened to her. I believe she pulled me back from the brink of Anorexia.

The same year, my third year of high school, I was exhibiting signs of anxiety. My eating was definitely problematic, even if I didn't have full-blown Anorexia. I had started to be a perfectionist in my schoolwork. For example, I would tear up a whole foolscap page of handwriting if I wasn't satisfied with the look of the very last word. Then I re-wrote it. My handwriting had become miniscule as well, and I had to almost have my nose on the paper to read it.

The other anxiety-related symptom I had in high school was migraine headaches. At the time, no-one linked my migraines to anxiety. They didn't know I had anxiety. The headaches were debilitating, and I had to take time off school. Interestingly, Mum's mother had been a migraine sufferer, but I don't know that anyone made the connection. Nana used to miss out on events because she would get a migraine. My father had also suffered from headaches, but I don't know if they were migraines.

As I recall this time in my life, I ask myself, 'What did we do for fun?' We retreated whenever possible to the holiday house at Binningup in the South West of WA. There, we would get away from the pressures of school and work. The house was set in a citrus orchard surrounded by bush. We would go for walks in the bush, go to the beach and just chill on the property. I have very fond memories of holidays at Binningup.

My sister and I were very fortunate to have a mother who valued travelling. She took us on a cruise around the Pacific Islands and to Europe. The Europe trip happened at the end of 1976. We flew to London, where we joined the rest of the tour group. My sister and I were the youngest passengers by far. Mum and my sister shared a room, and I shared with another young woman. That arrangement ended in tears part way across Europe.

It was Winter, as that was the only time available in the school year for a long trip. We flew to Paris and started a bus tour of France, Italy, Germany, and the Netherlands, to name a few countries. In Paris, Mum woke up on the morning we were leaving and read her watch wrongly. She woke my sister, thinking that they had slept in. My sister ran down to the room I was sharing and tried to wake me up. I was sound asleep and probably had my head under the covers as the other girl insisted on having the window open. Back in their room, Mum had changed and heated up their croissants, which they hastily ate. They were a bit mystified that no one else had put their suitcases out for collection. That's when they realised that it was only 2.10 am!

It was a busy two weeks. At Genoa in Italy, there was an unfortunate incident with my roommate. As soon as we arrived at our hotel, I ran a bath so I could wash my hair, which badly needed it. However, I realised that the shampoo was in Mum's room, and she had gone for a walk with my sister and my room mate. Immediately after she returned, I went up the corridor to get the shampoo. On the way back to my room, I suddenly had a thought that my room mate was in the bath I had run for myself. Sure enough, I opened the door and heard her splashing in the tub. I was incensed!

I immediately turned around and fled back to Mum and my sister. It was a knee-jerk reaction, not a rational response. I'm not sure what triggered me, but I was very upset. I certainly felt put upon. Maybe I was immature, sheltered and intolerant. Whatever the reason, I didn't share with that girl after that night.

After two weeks in Europe, we returned to England and visited some of Grandpa's relatives on Hayling Island. He was the third eldest of ten children in his family. We stayed with his sister Marjorie, who lived by herself, having never married. On the day we arrived, she put a chicken in the oven to roast. Before it was fully cooked, she took it out because we wouldn't have time to eat it that day. The chicken was left on the bench overnight. The next day, she put the chicken back in the oven but still didn't finish cooking it that day. On the third day, the chicken was served for supper. How we didn't get food poisoning, I don't know.

My sister and I were sharing a bed, and it had an electric blanket. We got into bed and instantly jumped back out again, like two cartoon characters. It was boiling hot, and we nearly got burnt. We didn't know our Great Aunt had left the electric blanket on the highest setting for three days because she thought we Australians would be cold. Luckily, it didn't catch on fire and burn the house down.

My sister and I were very fortunate to have that experience with Mum. Apart from all the wonderful cities we visited and the culture we were exposed to, we had precious time with her alone. That was a true gift because we didn't get as much time with our mother by ourselves as we would have liked. Many teenagers want to get away from their parents, but we wanted to have Mum all to ourselves. With Grandpa living there, we had to share her. Occasionally, our aunt would take Grandpa to her place for the afternoon. However, our Grandpa-free time was more often than not short-lived because they had had an argument, and she brought him home.

In my final year of high school, I was conscientious and studious. I didn't have a social life outside the family, unlike some of my friends. Reflecting on this time in my life, I can see I was quite sheltered. Mum, my sister and I were very close, and some people took us for sisters rather than mother and daughters.

I finished school at 17 and obtained a good score in my university entrance exams. That enabled me to secure a place in the course I wanted – teaching. In 1977, there were limited options for girls. Teaching was an obvious choice for me for several reasons. My mother and her two sisters were also teachers. I came from a family of teachers. When I was little, before I even went to kindergarten, I used to play school with my dolls as my students. Later, in Primary school, I used to 'mark' my birthday card with a red pen.

When I left school, I thought I was grown up. In reality, I was far from it. I knew very little about the world. My twelve years of school education had filled my brain with book knowledge, some of which I would never use again. For example, I haven't solved one quadratic equation since leaving school over 40 years ago.

What did I know at 17? I certainly knew what grief felt like. I knew what compromise and capitulation meant. However, I knew very little about myself, my potential and what I really wanted to do with my life. The concept of a gap year didn't exist then, so I went straight into further education. It never occurred to me to question the assumption that I would continue my formal education.

At 17, having grown up in a very small family and attended a single-sex school, I was completely ignorant about boys. I didn't even have any male cousins. My world was pretty much female. It was also restricted. Looking back, it was rather a sad situation for a young woman. Deep down, I would have loved to have a social life and the opportunity to meet boys, but I had no idea how to make it happen.

Through circumstances beyond my control, I was a relatively late bloomer in terms of relationships with the opposite sex. My father wasn't alive to show me how men would treat me as a woman. The older I got, the more I felt that loss. I missed not knowing my father as I entered the next phase of my life.

Chapter 4

Independent Career Woman

In the late 1970s, the career options for females were limited. Teaching and nursing were the main professions promoted to them. For me, teaching was an obvious choice as my mother and her two sisters had all been teachers. As a young child in pre-school, I used to play schools with my dolls. When I was in Primary School, I used to pretend to be a teacher by 'marking' my birthday cards with a red pen. You could say I was destined to be a teacher.

I was just 17 when I commenced teacher training, and I still lived at home. Apart from travelling, I had little life experience to bring to my role as a teacher. Since the mid-2010s in Australia, a few universities have made teaching a post-graduate qualification, a move that makes sense to me. I feel I would definitely have benefited from taking a break from education settings. By the time I had finished my studies, I had spent 16 years in schools, from kindergarten to teachers' college.

The first four years of my teaching career were spent in country schools. The first was a District High School with an Agricultural High School attached. It was situated in the Wheatbelt, East of Perth. Coincidentally, my mother was born in this area and spent the first ten years of her life in the neighbouring town. My introduction to school teaching was a 'baptism by fire' and not at all what I expected.

The Ag School, as it was known, was home-away-from-home for students aged between 15 and 17. About twelve of the students were female, so there were two female supervisors. Newly appointed Secondary teachers were expected to fill the role if there was a vacancy. In return for board and lodging, but no additional pay, the supervisors were required to be in charge of students out of school hours, including weekends.

In retrospect, I was too inexperienced to take on a substitute parent role straight out of teachers' college. I was way out of my depth, and I really did not want to be in that environment. I resented the restrictions imposed on me by the role. For example, some weekends, I had to be on duty with one other supervisor from 4 pm Friday afternoon to Monday morning. That meant I couldn't leave the property and had to eat all my meals with the students.

Writing this, I question why I didn't just resign from the job and return to Perth. It was my paradigm that told me to stay because, after all, I studied for three years to obtain my qualification. There was also the very strong message I had received repeatedly as a child. Growing up, I was told that my father had always wanted to raise Hereford cattle in the South

West of WA. As his mother had disapproved, he had instead become an accountant in a printing company.

Whenever I heard that story, I felt sad for my father. His mother had dominated his life, and he wasn't able to stand up to her. He didn't follow his dreams. Decades later, I was doing a similar thing by continuing in a job I didn't like because that was what was expected. At the beginning of my second year, I really didn't want to go back to work after the long holidays and expressed my feelings to Mum.

Mum, part of the Builder generation, had a stoic approach to life. Whatever happened, you just had to suck it up and get on with it. It wasn't that she didn't understand me, she just didn't have any other advice to give me. For example, she reminded me that I had a beautiful new car to drive back, a car that I could afford to buy with the money I was earning in my job. Like my father before me, I did what was expected.

At the end of the year, I was delighted to get a transfer to a Senior High School on the south coast of WA. It was about an eight-hour drive from Perth. It was a very happy day when I drove out of the Ag School campus for the last time. I felt free.

Living a long way away from Perth and my family gave me my first real taste of independence. I lived in a government teachers' accommodation with another teacher. When she moved out part way through the year, I had the place to myself, and I relished it. For example, I decorated the kitchen wall with a clear shower curtain that looked like a window with pot plants. In my bedroom, I somehow attached a poster to the ceiling and furnished the lounge room with a papasan chair.

The two years I spent working and living in that town were the first time I really did feel independent. The distance from the city and my family allowed me to be me and make my own decisions. I didn't have to answer to anyone else, and it was liberating.

I had some interesting experiences in those two years. One night, I literally saw something out of this world. The girl I was sharing with woke me up in the middle of the night, 'Come and look at this.' Half asleep, I went into the front bedroom and saw a light in the street leading up to the unit. 'She got me up to look at a light in the street?' I thought, and went back to bed. A little while later, I got up again to get a drink. By then, there was no longer a light in the street, but there were two lights up in the sky, moving together. Was it a UFO? Maybe, is all I can say.

I have fond memories of living in that town, the people I met and the opportunities I took. One such opportunity was amateur theatre. I doubt I would have pursued this opportunity, but it fell in my lap, so to speak. The director of one of the plays was also an English teacher at the high school where I worked, and she asked me to help backstage. It was something totally out of my comfort zone, and I really enjoyed it.

The next step in my teaching career was a transfer back to Perth and a large city high school. I was very happy to be back in the city. There wasn't much night life in the country town I lived in, and I was ready to party and let my hair down.

That year, I met some men and went out on dates, which was fun. However, I was totally unaware of my subconscious fear of abandonment. Like my father many years before, I thought that every man I liked would leave me, and that is just what happened. I didn't understand what I was doing wrong, or why the same pattern repeated itself.

I had met a few men while living in the country but didn't form any long-term relationships. Maybe that was because I didn't want to stay in the country, and I definitely didn't see myself as a farmer's wife. Back then, in my early twenties, I had no idea what sort of man I wanted to be with, or what qualities I was looking for in a prospective partner. I didn't have a type of man I preferred. So, I tended to go for men who noticed me, and made the first move.

I can see now that was an indication of my low self-esteem and my lack of experience with men. Mum would tell me, 'Don't chase men', but I thought that was old-fashioned advice. At nightclubs, I would approach men and talk to them. I wasn't backward in coming forward, so to speak. I liked that about myself, that I was confident to talk to men, to make the first move. I thought I was a modern, empowered woman.

More often than not, I was disappointed. Just when I thought things were going well, I was enjoying going out with a man, the phone calls stopped. The excuses started, the pulling back started. One guy I went out with for a few months broke my heart when he just up and left the state. He sent me a postcard of all things to tell me that he had to leave Perth on business.

At the end of 1985, I met the man I eventually married. During that year, I had had some highs and lows in relationships. I had had my heart broken, and I maybe broke a heart too. There was one guy who was very keen on me, but I'm afraid I didn't see a future with him. In my mind, the relationship wasn't going to work because he didn't have the same level of formal education as I had. That was my belief system at the time.

The man I met at a ballroom dancing studio was unlike any other man I had ever met. He was quiet and reserved. I admired his intelligence and that he had a university education. I thought that meant we were compatible and could have interesting conversations. What I had no awareness of was my familiarity with emotionally unavailable men. Both my father and grandfather had been emotionally unavailable for different reasons, so that's what I was comfortable with.

At the end of 1985, when I met my Mr Right, I was working full-time as a Teacher Librarian in a large metropolitan high school. I was studying for a Bachelor of Education. Life was good, and I was very happy. Although I had years of formal education, I was completely unaware of my paradigms, the subconscious conditioning that was running my life. School had taught me nothing about myself.

Now that I am aware of my paradigms, I can see my behaviour in the relationship with my then boyfriend more clearly. I was passive. I didn't know how to be assertive and ask for what I wanted. One night, fairly soon after he moved in with me, I was preparing dinner by myself in the kitchen. While we were dating, he would talk to me while I made dinner. I asked him to come and talk to me, but he was more interested in his book. Once dinner was in the oven, I walked into the lounge room, snatched the book out of his hands and threw it across the room.

I was acting like a hurt little girl who wanted her Dad's attention and felt that she had to fight for it. However, I couldn't see that. My behaviour didn't have the desired result because my boyfriend was cross about the way I had treated his book. That was the pattern of our relationship for years. I pushed my needs down as long as I could, just like I did as a child, until I could suppress them no longer. One little thing, seemingly insignificant, would cause all the pent-up frustration and hurt to burst out.

At the time, I didn't know that my childhood trauma was playing out. I was triggered by his behaviour and believed I was being shut out, and that I wasn't important. Unfortunately, anger was something that he couldn't handle, and he wanted to shut it down as soon as possible. We weren't very good at communicating about issues.

I was unconsciously behaving in the same way I had with my father and grandfather. Except now, I was a grown woman who was doing what she could to keep the man happy. That was her job, after all. Countless times, I told myself, 'In the greater scheme of things, it isn't that important.' However, all those seemingly unimportant things that I tolerated and overlooked added up. They did matter, and, at times, I felt very resentful.

As time moved on, our relationship wasn't marred by constant arguments. That was largely because I was an expert people-pleaser. I just backed off, and took the path of least resistance time and time again. It was my default position, but it wasn't healthy at all. I just couldn't see it then.

As a girl, I had always envisioned myself as married. Whenever I bought a toy ring with my pocket money, I would put it on my ring finger when no one was looking. I don't think I had my wedding all planned out like some girls, but it was definitely something I wanted one day.

One day in 1988, when we were talking about the house we were planning to build, I brought up the idea of getting married. In the past, we had agreed that when we built our house, we would get married. According to tradition, a woman can propose in a Leap Year, so I did. If I had waited for him to propose, I probably would've still been waiting.

Chapter 5
Married Life

We married in April, 1989. It was a small, intimate wedding with the reception at my mother's home. The day dawned with howling gales and driving rain, the result of a rare tropical cyclone reaching Perth. By the time we left for the church, the weather had fined up, and eventually the temperature reached 37 degrees. That wasn't supposed to happen.

Our marriage lasted 22 years, so by then, I had been with the one man for a quarter of a century. It's not possible to condense all those years into one chapter, but now that I have been apart from him for eleven years, I can see the relationship from a wider perspective.

Children came along early in our marriage. Maybe that was the reason we met and married; to bring our two daughters into the world. They are the best thing to have come out of the marriage for me. Our firstborn came into the world after a difficult pregnancy, during which I was hospitalised for the last five weeks.

As the weeks passed, I felt increasingly isolated. I was acutely aware that this was the last time my husband

and I would have without children, and we had to be apart, which made me sad. Even though we wanted to be parents, our lives were going to change, and that time was precious to me at least. The other thing that made me sad was that my husband didn't visit me as often as I would have liked. When he did visit, he seemed keen to leave. Hospitals made him feel very uncomfortable for some reason.

With the benefit of hindsight, that was a huge red flag. However, at the time, neither of us knew what was ahead and how much time we'd be involved with hospitals. There was no way I could prepare myself emotionally for the journey ahead.

The events of the day she was born are permanently etched in my memory. I think I spent the whole day crying. When I was being wheeled into the operating theatre, I was terrified that I wasn't numb enough. I remember the anaesthetist trying to make me laugh as the procedure started. My husband was beside me, decked out in green hospital scrubs.

As soon as our daughter was delivered, she was shown briefly to me before being rushed to the Neonatal Intensive Care Unit in a humidicrib. It was unreal, like something out of a medical drama on TV. While I was being stitched up, my husband went with her and returned to me with a polaroid photo of our baby girl.

The first week of our daughter's life was very stressful. She was born with Hyaline Membrane Disease, and stiff lungs, due to prematurity. Her weight was 1935 grams. I couldn't hold her or breastfeed her as she was too tiny. The first time my husband and I could hold her was when she was about four days old.

I was catapulted into a foreign world and just had to navigate my way through it, largely by myself. My husband didn't take any time off work, so it was all up to me. I was on a steep learning curve, talking to doctors, nurses and learning how to express my milk using a machine that closely resembled a milking machine. It was nothing like I imagined my early days as a mother would be.

After a week, I went home but had to leave my baby in hospital. That was very hard to do. My husband didn't pick me up from the hospital; Mum did. And she also took me to hospital every day to see my daughter because I couldn't drive.

As I write this, it is incomprehensible how little my husband involved himself in his newborn's life. He left it to me, and, of course, I picked up the whole responsibility. Even on weekends, when he could have come with me, he opted out. He just couldn't face the hospital environment. It wasn't easy for me, either, but wild horses wouldn't have kept me away.

Our second daughter was born three and a half years later. The pregnancy, fortunately, was much easier, and she went full term before being born by caesarean. We need not have thought about boys' names, because all the men at my husband's workplace fathered girls. Our daughter, from memory, was the 26th girl born in a four-year period.

Prior to having our daughters, we hadn't discussed how we were going to raise them. I had decided that I was going to read to my children from the day they were born. He had decided that he didn't want to be the same sort of father that he had had; not showing affection or telling his children they were loved. I commend him for that, as I have often said to our daughters.

As parents, we were not on the same page. For example, one night while putting our older daughter to bed, I sang to her, 'Hush little baby, don't you cry, Mama's going to buy you a mockingbird. And if that mockingbird don't sing, Papa's going to buy you a diamond ring…' When I came back into the living room, he said, 'Don't sing that song to her. She'll think that when anything breaks, someone will buy her something new.' I was flabbergasted, 'It's just a song!' but he was serious.

Countless times, I wasn't assertive enough in the face of his behaviour. It didn't get me the results I wanted, which was discussion and agreement on how we raised the girls. One example of this was the evening meal. In my family of origin, we had always eaten 'tea' at the dining room table, and the TV wasn't on. My husband's family treated mealtimes as purely an opportunity to re-fuel. It wasn't a social occasion as in my family.

I recall one instance where my husband ignored the rest of the family, left the table and turned on the TV in the adjoining family room. My younger daughter called her father out, 'Dad, we haven't finished our dinner.' His reply was, 'Well, I have, and I'm watching the news.' End of discussion.

I learned through experience that if I complained about my husband's behaviour after the event, I would be dismissed, and accused of trying to pick a fight. In his words, 'There's nothing wrong with me. If you have a problem, it's in your head. You're choosing to see it that way.' No responsibility taken, no apology. In fact, my husband never apologised to me in our whole marriage.

I stopped expressing anger because my husband couldn't handle it.

I stopped wearing perfume, because it made him sneeze.

I stopped bringing flowers into the house for the same reason.

In short, I stopped being the me I was when we met; independent and confident. It was a slow process. I had stopped growing, and was living my life according to someone else's expectations. What I was really doing was reverting to the way I had lived at home with my father and grandfather. I had chosen, subconsciously, an emotionally unavailable man because that was what I was used to.

I believe that relationships are jointly created by the two people involved. The relationship provides a context in which each person can express themselves. Our relationship was created mostly subconsciously, but I don't think we were alone in that. We both lacked awareness of our own emotional baggage, so we brought it into the marriage.

My heaviest piece of emotional baggage was my subconscious fear of abandonment. My self-esteem, especially in relation to men, was low. That led me to tolerate and excuse behaviour from my husband that wasn't loving. I didn't feel loved in the way I wanted to be loved as a wife and a woman.

I had a fear of history repeating itself. I dreaded my husband dying young, just like my father, and leaving me to raise two children by myself. Until my husband passed the age that my father had been, 43, and my children passed the ages my sister and I had been at the time, 11 and 9, I unknowingly held my breath. I didn't want my children to suffer the grief of losing their father and growing up without his presence.

In the 1980's, the first decade of our relationship, there was no understanding of Asperger's Syndrome. I just thought his behaviour was the result of his upbringing. It would have helped enormously to understand that I was possibly entering into a neurodiverse marriage where one person was 'on the spectrum' and the other wasn't.

The first I heard about it was from a neighbour who was a Special Needs teacher. She suggested that my husband might have it as she could see traits in his behaviour. By then, we had been together for ten years. I can't say if he is 'on the Spectrum' and he hasn't been diagnosed. However, from what I have read and understand, it could explain some of his behaviour.

Going into the relationship equipped with knowledge and skills to deal effectively with communication issues would have helped both of us. Instead, I was continually trying to 'get through' to someone who wasn't able to hear me on an emotional level. He would stonewall my efforts to discuss anything important. Once, when I wanted to talk about our different attitudes to money, he crossed his arms and turned his body away from me. That said it all, no words were needed.

As a result of being shut down, I pushed my feelings down. I told myself repeatedly, 'In the greater scheme of things, it's not that important.' That wasn't true, but it was my habit from childhood to suppress my feelings to keep other people happy.

Occasionally, my husband would use a tone of voice that took me right back to my childhood. For example, if he came into the kitchen and found the cat food on the bench, he would demand to know, 'Who left the tuna out?' If it was me, he would refuse to put the tuna back in the fridge because then I wouldn't learn not to leave it out. He would go on and on until I stopped what I was doing and attended to it. Why did I put up with that? It was my habit and low self-esteem.

Just like my grandfather, my husband would act on an idea without considering how it might impact other people. One time, we were preparing to go on a short holiday with our two-year-old. Mum had come over to look after our daughter so we could concentrate on the packing. Out of the blue, my husband decided to make a batch of scones to take on the trip, messing up the kitchen and delaying our departure. Mum was furious with him and said. 'I hope you choke on them!'

Another time, on the day of our daughter's christening, he decided to mount the clothes dryer on the wall in the laundry. The dryer, in the corner of the dining room, had been disguised with a tablecloth, carefully pinned into place for the post-christening afternoon tea. That was flung on the floor. I returned from having my hair done to find the laundry in a mess. 'Don't you want the dryer on the wall?', he asked. 'Yes, but it doesn't have to be today!' There was nothing I could do but seethe with frustration because he had made up his mind to do the job then and there.

The beliefs I held, subconsciously, about the role of a married woman and mother led me to take on far more than I could cope with in the long term. After Dad died, I saw Mum have to juggle raising children, working, running the house and caring. She kept all those balls in the air and didn't let my sister and I see the toll it took on her. She was my role model.

Several times during the marriage, my mental health deteriorated, and anxiety brought me to an abrupt halt.

As Gabor Maté, author of *When The Body Says 'No'*[3] observed, my body was telling me to take a break in the only way it knew how. As was my habit, I kept adding on responsibilities, thinking I could do it all. I obviously couldn't. That year, my aunt was dying from breast cancer, I had two young children, was working casually outside the home, and my husband was working long hours.

Gradually, I got my anxiety levels under control with the help of medication. In the process, I hadn't learned anything about how the mind works and my habit of taking on too much. Headaches, like I had suffered as a teenager, returned and lasted several days at a time. They were debilitating, and the only thing I could do was rest. My daughters would ask me, 'Do you have a headache, Mum? You have your headache voice on.' I would sleep for hours on weekends because, at least when I was asleep, no one could ask me to do anything.

My habit of taking on too much persisted for many years. I wouldn't have known how to change it anyway. Although I couldn't see it at the time, the more I did for the family, the less my husband did. Out of curiosity, one day, I asked my daughters, 'How do you see my role in the family?' Without hesitation, my younger daughter said, 'You're the one who does everything.' She was right.

---

[3] Gabor Maté, *When the Body Says No: The Cost of Hidden Stress*, Melbourne, Scribe, 2003

As my daughters grew older, they were so fortunate to have a father who gave them hugs and told them he loved them. He would stop working to watch *Dr Who* or *Stargate* with them, as they all loved science fiction and fantasy. I was hurt because, as his wife, I didn't receive hugs and 'I love you'. It was like I was invisible to him. Occasionally, I would wave my hand in front of his face and remind him, 'It gets awfully lonely on Earth while you're in cyberspace!'

It was only later that the realisation dawned on me; I was jealous because I didn't have my dad when I was a teenager. I would dearly loved to have had hugs from my dad, but it wasn't to be, and there was nothing I could do about it.

The end of the marriage was not sudden; it was ten years in the making. During that time, my husband returned to university full-time to earn a PhD, and my mother developed Alzheimer's disease. Those two circumstances eventually spelled the end of the marriage, at least for me. As well as working every afternoon, running the house, and mothering, I helped my sister care for our mother at home. Meanwhile, my husband studied.

I really shouldn't have been surprised that my husband couldn't deal with my mother's illness. 'If I couldn't use my brain, life wouldn't be worth living,' he maintained. 'I happen to think a person is more than their brain', I responded. So he did what he'd always done when he couldn't face something; buried his head in work. He was not prepared to support me practically or emotionally through what turned out to be a long journey. In the next chapter, I will reflect on my journey as a carer.

The final year of the marriage was also my younger daughter's final year of school. Although I wanted to leave, it wouldn't have been fair to pull the rug out from under her. I stayed for one more year, during which I sought the help of an excellent male psychologist who helped me understand that what I was asking for in the marriage – attention, affection and support were perfectly normal in the context of a marriage. My husband had told me repeatedly, over the years, that I was 'needy' and that my happiness was my own responsibility.

I used to think that it was a cop-out on his part to tell me that. Wouldn't a husband want to contribute to his wife's happiness? It's only been in the course of writing this book that I have had cause to reflect on that idea. Now, I see it differently. I always had the power in the relationship to be happy; I just lacked the awareness. I chose to stay, chose to put my needs on the bottom of my list of priorities. However, I wasn't doing it consciously. Given my upbringing, I was making the only decision I knew how to make.

The end of the marriage, when I finally stood up for myself and spoke my truth, came immediately after my daughter finished school. In a coffee shop, I expressed the opinion that now both of our daughters had finished school, we had time to do more together as a couple. It was made very clear to me that work was my husband's priority, not our relationship. On the way home, I tried to talk about our relationship, but he walked off saying, 'I'm not going to discuss our dirty laundry in public'. I walked home, alone and in tears, knowing that it was over.

There were a lot of tears on my part. I was so sad for it to end, even though it wasn't healthy and hadn't been for a long time. Part of me was proud of myself because I had finally taken the step that I needed to take. I had finally reclaimed my power. I was finally taking responsibility for my own happiness.

Chapter 6
The Sandwich Generation

Before the term 'sandwich generation', was introduced into popular culture, my mother was part of it; a pioneer in a way. With two daughters to raise and elderly parents to care for, she had a heavy load. Unfortunately, her younger sister wasn't supportive or very helpful. For example, after Dad died, I remember feeling excited when my aunt visited on her way home from work. She'd have a cup of tea and then make an excuse to leave. She never stayed very long.

Even as a young girl, my aunt's behaviour made an impression on me. I didn't understand why her visits were so short as she wasn't yet married and lived by herself. When my grandfather came to live with us, she wasn't supportive of Mum, in my opinion. Occasionally, she would take Grandpa to her place for lunch, giving Mum, my sister, and me time to ourselves. Alas, our freedom would be curtailed way too early because they had had an argument, and she brought him home.

Years later, when Mum became ill with Alzheimer's, I determined that I was going to support my sister in whatever way I could. I used to give my sister and brother-in-law a break on the weekends during the football season by staying with Mum. She couldn't be left alone at all. The conversation was very repetitive; Mum's short-term memory was shot. It went something like this, 'Well, we'd better go then,' said Mum. I would reply, 'They've gone to the football. We're staying here.' 'Ok. Well, we'd better go then,' Mum said a minute later.

I had learnt, from my own research into caring for a person with dementia, that it was best to answer the questions the same way each time. Mum didn't know that she was repeating herself; she couldn't retain new memories. To her, every utterance was new. Even with that understanding and deep reservoirs of patience, it was draining.

As soon as I walked in the door, someone would ask me, 'What's for dinner?' I just had to go and decompress for a while before I could think about dinner. I don't recall my daughters or husband enquiring about how my visit had gone. They had no idea how hard it was to keep saying the same thing. I would have appreciated their company and support, but it was not forthcoming. My husband's attitude was, 'The girls shouldn't have to go to their grandmother's if they don't want to.'

There was no moving him from that position. Intellectually, I understood that he couldn't face Mum's mental deterioration; it might happen to him one day too. Emotionally, I felt unsupported, just like when my older daughter was a baby. I was trying to show my daughters what caring looks like; love in action. It was what Mum had shown me throughout my life, after all.

I clearly remember driving her home one day when she thanked me for 'being very kind'. Writing this, I realise she probably didn't recognise me as her grown-up daughter Heather. My reply was, 'Well, you were the one who taught me how to care.' I'm very grateful to her for showing me what care looked like in its various forms.

In the early days of Mum's Alzheimer's journey, I felt incredibly torn between my family of origin and the one I had created. I was trying to process my grief over the changes in Mum; she was struggling, and it was heartbreaking to watch. One day, we were doing some embroidery, and she kept asking me, 'Is this ok?'. It wasn't nearly up to her usual standard, and I think she knew that. She never would have checked with me in the past. After all, Mum had hand-embroidered tiny roses on my daughters' baby clothes and hand-smocked dresses for them.

One year, Mum and I helped make costumes for the Christmas concert at the girls' school. Mum had been a Home Economics teacher at that school for many years. I was very surprised that Mum wasn't able to work out how to cut the fabric, something she could have done with her eyes closed when I was growing up. I didn't understand that this was an early symptom of something seriously wrong.

Inevitably, the illness progressed, and it became clear that Mum wasn't safe by herself. One school holidays, my sister and brother-in-law were away on holidays, and Mum wasn't coping at all well. I called in each morning, and she looked very worried. 'I couldn't work out how to lock the door last night', she told me, so she probably hadn't slept much. The cat's bowl was full of chocolate biscuits. As I was going with my husband and daughters to his aunt's farm, I felt I had no choice but to take her with me.

It was during that holiday that I saw both how much help Mum needed and how my husband couldn't cope. He kept leaving me with Mum, and taking the girls into the nearby town or for walks around the farm. Poor Mum couldn't understand why her granddaughters didn't want to spend time with her. She could feel it, maybe more keenly than me. I was furious when he told her, to her face, 'You can't look after yourself.' Mum was in floods of tears, and I tried to comfort her without much success. In private, I asked him, 'What gives you the right to say that?' Already, I was taking on an advocacy role for Mum. I shouldn't have had to advocate for her with my husband.

If I could re-live that time in my life, with my current level of awareness, I would try to negotiate a plan for supporting my mother with my husband. It would have been a very different experience with his support.

However, it's not possible to go back in time. As I see the situation now, I had a deeply embedded belief that I would not receive emotional or practical support from any man in my life. I just didn't know I had it. On a conscious level, I wanted the support and asked for it, but I wasn't coming from a place of certainty. Therefore, I didn't get the support. The Universe was giving me what I believed I would receive.

Early in our family's journey with dementia, I remember attending counselling from Alzheimer's Australia. In floods of tears, I poured out my distress over being pulled in two directions at once. On the one hand, were my husband and daughters. On the other was my mother and sister. I loved them all. Everyone needed me, but I couldn't be in two places at the same time. Still, I tried to please everyone as I was used to doing.

I will never know for sure why Mum got Alzheimer's disease, but I have my own theory. It's natural to wonder why something unexpected happened, but at some point along the way, I put that question aside. In its place, I came to an acceptance. I couldn't change the diagnosis and the slow decline in Mum's cognitive abilities, but I *did* have a choice in how I responded. I could have crawled into the foetal position, pulled a blanket over my head and lived in fear. The other choice was to adopt an attitude of acceptance of what was in front of me. That was the choice I made, and it allowed me to see the gifts in the situation.

What were those gifts? Patience was an important one, patience to answer the same question every few minutes without giving way to frustration. Another gift was living in the present, giving all my attention to the task at hand. When I was feeding Mum her morning tea or lunch, I had to concentrate on what I was doing. It was both something practical I could do for her, as well as something I never imagined I would have to do; spoon feed my mother like a baby.

As I've related in this book, Mum spent a lot of time caring for other people, both in the family and the general community. There was my father, who had struggled with his mental health during their marriage, her sister who had cancer, her nephew who also had mental illness. She volunteered her time and skills to a number of organisations during her lifetime. I've described how Mum supported me when my older daughter was born prematurely. When she was six months old, Mum joined the hospital auxiliary service and collected knitted garments for premature babies.

I have often wondered if my mother wanted to experience the loving care she had given to family and strangers herself. Illness was a way to achieve it. No one would *consciously* choose to develop Alzheimer's disease with all the loss it entails. Maybe she wanted to forget the pain she had endured during her adult life. The pain of losing her husband way earlier than she ever would have expected, having to bring up her daughters single-handedly, losing her younger sister to cancer at 65 years. She once said to me, 'Life wasn't much fun.' How sad.

Another reason was that Mum was suddenly widowed in her early 40's in tragic circumstances. It was a huge shock to be left behind to raise two daughters who were still in primary school. Due to societal norms in Australia in the early 1970s, she believed that she had to hide the truth from my sister and me about how our father died. I believe the burden of having to keep the family secret weighed heavily on Mum. How could it not?

One of the fairly early symptoms of Mum's illness was aphasia, the inability to speak and understand spoken language. I firmly believe that it was no accident that aphasia occurred along with the deterioration in her memory. If she forgot that she had to keep the family secret, we wouldn't be able to understand what she was trying to tell us. At times, her speech was so incomprehensible that we didn't know how to respond.

I was part of the sandwich generation for about fifteen years. It was a long time to watch my mother's condition deteriorate slowly, unstoppably. Along the way, I was incredibly fortunate to be able to work with my sister in caring for Mum. I say fortunate because families are often torn apart by dementia, and siblings don't always work together. There were times we didn't see eye to eye either, but that's to be expected.

Chapter 7
The Awakening Begins

Throughout my adult life, I read many self-help books, gathering information on relationships, health and spirituality. I read John Gray's *Men Are From Mars, Women Are from Venus*,[4] Neale Donald Walsch's *Conversations with God*[5] and Harville Hendrick's *Getting The Love You Want*[6], amongst the most memorable. What I didn't understand, because school and university hadn't taught me, was that learning was more than gathering information through reading.

It took leaving Perth, my family and friends, and everything familiar to begin what I refer to as my *real* education. I had to get right out of my comfort zone to grow. 'You're so brave' was a comment I often heard when I told people I was moving to Melbourne. I didn't see myself as brave; I was just very excited.

---

[4] John Gray, Men are From Mars, Women Are From Venus, Thorsons, London, 1993
[5] Neale Donald Walsch, *Conversations With God: An Uncommon Dialogue*, Book 1, Sydney, Hodder, 1996.
[6] Harville Hendrix, PHD, *Getting the Love You Want. A Guide For Couples*, Holt & Co, New York, 1988.

The Awakening Begins

Wild horses couldn't have kept me from fulfilling my dream.

At fifty seven, I was still ignorant of my true nature; I just had a glimpse of what I could create in my life. Although I told myself, 'After moving to Melbourne, I can achieve anything I set my mind to', I didn't really believe it. I let self-doubt fill my mind when I wasn't able to find a job in health promotion and experienced high levels of anxiety.

It was only a few months after moving to Melbourne that I discovered Bob Proctor, one of the leaders in the personal development industry. At the time, I was studying life coaching, and a remark by the presenter really struck me. 'If you think coaching is worthwhile, why wouldn't you have a coach yourself.' It made sense, so I went off to find a coach. That's how I found Bob Proctor.

In August 2018, I began the year-long coaching program, which, for the very first time, taught me how the mind works. I was, and still am, flabbergasted that I knew nothing about that until I was 57! 'Why wasn't I taught about the mind at teachers' college and university?', I asked myself. It would have helped me as a parent as well.

Over the last five years since arriving in Melbourne, I have been re-inventing myself, and I like myself much better for it. For a start, I am no longer a card-carrying people pleaser. If I don't want to do something, I'm comfortable saying an emphatic 'no'. I have found 'no' to be a liberating word.

I can clearly see the change in several areas of my life, relationships, career and money. In 2019, I met a man called Paul. I had to come all the way across the country to meet the man who I now share my life with. Unlike the way I was in my marriage, I am assertive and have strong boundaries. I respect myself enough to ask for what I want and need. In return, I am seen and heard by my partner, which makes me feel loved.

Studying Bob Proctor's material has resulted in a fundamental change in my view of education and learning. When I was at school and university, learning meant getting the facts and being able to show I could remember them in an essay or some other assessment. There was no experiential component, which meant I hadn't internalised the learning.

Now, I have a much wider definition of education that involves changing behaviour. I am no longer satisfied with understanding ideas intellectually. I want to understand them experientially, and live them. One thing I have learnt from experience is the power of gratitude, not only for what is in my life now but for what I am creating. I have been keeping a daily gratitude journal for several years. Writing down and *feeling* what I am grateful for every day brings more wonderful people and opportunities into my life. This book goes on my daily list.

The way I approach my life now is completely different from the past. If I am considering undertaking a project, my first consideration is, 'Do I really want to do this?' In the past, that would definitely not have been my priority; the way I brought up, you did what you were expected to do, not what you wanted to do necessarily. My father had a dream to raise Hereford cattle in the Southwest of WA, but he never realised it. Sadly, it wasn't what he was expected to do, at least by his mother.

I've learned that when I undertake something without really wanting to do it, I end up disappointed. The most recent example of this was when I decided to do the Cambridge University English as a Second Language teaching certificate. I had been told that I needed it if I was to gain employment in the overseas student ESL sector. Interestingly, I ignored my gut instinct, telling me not to do any more training, 'Not another course!'. I did learn a lot from doing the first half of the course; just not what the trainers were intending. I didn't finish the course.

Sometimes, learning what you *don't* want puts you on the right path, the path to what you really do want. For me, it was deciding to start a business, coaching adults to speak English, using my own method. I've decided to work with older migrants, people who have been in Australia for many years but are not confident, or able to speak English fluently.

I've discovered that I am not comfortable sitting in 'boxes' constructed by other people, organisations, or society in general. Just because it's always been done a certain way, doesn't mean it is the right way for me to do it. No, I want to smash out of the box and do things a different way. There is more than one way to help adults speak English; one size doesn't fit everyone. Likewise, my way won't suit everyone.

Where did that rebellious streak come from? Possibly, I had an ancestor somewhere in the family tree who I take after. It could also be my Type 3 nature, according to Carol Tuttle's *Energy Profiling System*.[7] I discovered her shortly after leaving my marriage, and her work really impressed me. It helped me understand why I did things in a certain way.

In Carol Tuttle's *Energy Profiling System*, there are four Types, and she maintains that each of us is born leading with one Type although we have all four in unique proportions. An Energy Type describes how energy moves through a person and is expressed in facial features, the way the body is held, voice quality and behaviour. Using her quiz, I determined I was a Type 3, which helped me understand myself in a new, different way.

In Carol Tuttle's system, a Type 3 woman is described as rich and dynamic. It shows up in facial features such as my substantial nose, my uneven skin texture, and the way I hold my body. For example, I have a habit of tilting my head to one side when listening to a person in a conversation. I walk in a definite, determined way, and not always in a straight line.

Type 3 is extroverted in nature. People who lead with this Type often have their own business. They are organised and like to categorise things, which explains

---

[7] *Energy Type Quiz*, my.liveyourtruth.com

The Awakening Begins

my love of shops like Howard's Storage World. My ex-husband used to be amused by my tendency to organise clutter in baskets. I thought it was just my way of dealing with untidiness in the home. Energy Profiling showed me that it was an innate characteristic.

Growing up, my mother would say, 'I always know it's you coming up the front stairs.' My definite footfall gave me away. When we were walking down the street, she would ask, 'Can't you walk in a straight line?' as I zigzagged in front of her for the umpteenth time. It was my Type 3 nature shining through again. It was the same Type 3 energy that led me to ruin my sister's first birthday photo by suddenly shoving a handful of cake into her mouth.

There was nothing wrong with my Type 3 nature, but my parents didn't understand it. 'Slow down!'. 'Calm down!' I was admonished by parents who found my behaviour too much at times. I suspect that was mainly my father, particularly when he wasn't well. That's a pity, because it forced me to push it down and defer to my secondary Type 2 nature, concerned with people's comfort. In order to be a 'good girl', I had to be less of my true self.

By the time I learned about Energy Profiling, Mum was already in the nursing home with advanced Alzheimer's. It was very interesting to see that she was also a Type 3, judging by her facial features and behaviour. Looking closely at her face, I noticed one day that she had triangular nostrils; triangles are a Type 3 shape. She would also make angles with her body in the Type 3 way. On more than one visit, I walked into her room to see her lying flat on her back in bed with her arms crossed over her chest. Once I recovered from the shock of thinking she had died, I realised it was a very angular, Type 3 way to position her body.

Since discovering Carol Tuttle's work, I have shared her Energy Profiling quiz with many people. The point of the quiz is to determine your own Type and gain insights into your own behaviour. Over the years, I've learnt a lot about myself as a Type 3 woman, like my tendency to corral stuff into containers. I even do it with emails. The details of Carol Tuttle's Energy Profiling system are listed in the Appendix of this book.

Trying new things, and changing things up has always been fun for me. When I go to a hairdresser, I tell them to 'play' with my hair. My attitude is, 'If I don't like the result, it's only hair and will grow out'. As a young adult living away from home, I loved to change both my hairstyle and colour often. At one stage, I had a short, pixie-style haircut, coloured burgundy. I remember turning up to visit my mother the next day and her less than enthusiastic response. 'Oh,' she said. She didn't understand why I changed my hair so often and didn't like most of the changes.

Now, it's not only my hair that I change. I have gained the tools to change any aspect of my life whenever I want. That is very empowering! I have changed my habit of racing around, and get more done now that I live my life at a more relaxed pace. Even when I walk along the street, I walk at a moderate speed, although

I'm not sure if I walk in a straight line; maybe I never will achieve that.

Another habit that I have changed is the habit of living my life from the outside-in. That means that I rarely listen to the television news, read the newspaper, or engage in conversations about the state of the world. That doesn't mean I don't have opinions about what's going on, but I don't fill my mind with negative thoughts about situations I can't change. Instead, I think about the new business I'm launching to help older migrants speak English. I write my gratitude journal, listen to uplifting information, read books, knit for charity and spend time with my partner.

Earlier this year, I discovered the work of Gabor Maté on YouTube. The video was about the myth of the happy childhood; how many people think they had a happy childhood but were unaware of the trauma they suffered. I was one of those people. Since finding Dr Maté, I have read his book, *The Myth of Normal*[8] and told many people about his work. I have learnt that I was traumatised as a young child by having a father who was emotionally unavailable and who died when I was still a child. I suffered an emotional wound that pre-disposed me to the anxiety and depression I experienced as an adult.

The wounding wasn't intentional. My parents weren't to blame; they were doing the best they knew how with the awareness they had at the time. In the same

---

[8] Gabor Maté with Daniel Maté, *The Myth of Normal: Trauma, Illness and Healing in a Toxic Culture*, Vermillion, London, 2022

way, I wasn't to blame for how I inadvertently wounded my own children when I wasn't able to be available to them at times due to crippling levels of anxiety. I understood from Gabor Maté that what happened to me as a young child caused me to give up my real self in order to remain attached to my primary caregivers. In order to survive, attachment had to be the priority.

I am a committed life-long learner and am fascinated by human behaviour. There is an urge to constantly update my self-knowledge, and self-awareness. I read a lot and can't imagine not being a reader. New ideas appeal to me, and I think of myself as an early-adopter. For example, in the mid-2010s, I started Nordic walking, a form of exercise that developed from cross-country skiing. It didn't bother me that my daughters and husband wouldn't walk with me when I had my poles.

The opinions of other people don't determine what I do; I don't let them. Since studying Bob Proctor, I am no longer a card-carrying people pleaser. I have learnt to assert myself and not be the first person to give in when there's a difference of opinion. I live from the inside-out; set my own goals, and work towards them. Not all the time, not in every situation, certainly much more consistently than I used to do.

Chapter 8
The Family Secret

From A Different Perspective

In January 2011, at the age of fifty, I learnt the family secret that Mum had been guarding for several decades. The family secret was that my father had died by suicide, not a heart attack in his sleep, as I had believed since I was eleven.

I was visiting a family friend in Melbourne and talking about my mother. 'I don't think your mother ever got over your father's death', she commented. 'I don't think any of us did', I replied. His heart attack was so sudden.' Then she said, 'That's not what happened.' It was said quietly, gently. In that instant, before she told me what had really happened, I felt a huge wave of compassion wash over me for both my parents. I knew what she was going to say.

Our friend felt terrible because she didn't know that I didn't know the truth. After I left, she had rung my husband, mortified about what she had done. I think it's a good indication of the state of our marriage at the time, that he didn't call me to see if I was okay. My daughters weren't with me when I learnt the secret, and I was in shock when I got back to the hotel. I hadn't registered the enormity of what I had learnt.

Back home in Perth, I had to process the information. The only person I knew who could fill in the blanks for me was our next-door neighbour at the time. Her husband and my father had been good friends. Amazingly, she thought I should keep the information to myself since it happened so long ago. I wasn't prepared to keep the secret any longer. She didn't understand the consequences of being kept in the dark all our adult lives. 'How will it help to know?', she asked. 'I need to know what you know. I need to get it straight in my head,' I replied.

As the older sister, and the one who knew the secret, it was my responsibility to tell my sister. Sadly, it was another example of my husband not giving me the emotional support I needed and deserved. Although I had informed him that morning of my intention, when he returned from work, he asked, 'Did you have a nice day? 'No, I had to do one of the hardest things I ever had to do.' He had obviously forgotten what I had told him; maybe he just didn't listen.

I didn't receive a hug, offer of a cup of tea or anything in the way of comfort. It was times like that I felt very alone. The support my sister received was in stark contrast. Her husband took the afternoon off work to be with her. My husband just didn't seem capable of that; he couldn't empathise with me.

I was fortunate to have friends with whom I could confide. When I told one of my friends, she realised that she had been in the same hospital at the same time. She recalled overhearing the nurses talking amongst themselves about a 'tragic accident' that had occurred that morning. My friend Barbara said, 'I always thought there was something odd about that story', referring to my version of events the day Dad died.

To say it was a huge shock to learn that I had lived most of my life not knowing the truth about Dad's death is an understatement. It was hard not to wonder why I had been kept in the dark. I could completely understand why I wasn't told as a child; it was to protect me and my sister. That was a decision made out of love.

If I had been in Mum's position in 1971, what would I have told my young daughters? What could I have said that would help them understand that it wasn't their fault? I honestly don't know.

As a young girl, I had no reason to doubt what Mum told me. She was my mother; I loved and trusted her. I can still picture my sister, Mum, and I sitting around the kitchen table, all sobbing our hearts out. Dad was gone, and this time he wouldn't come back.

The family secret had long-term consequences that Mum couldn't have foreseen back in 1971. She couldn't have known that I would form a deep-seated belief that men in my life would suddenly disappear, just like my father had. I had a fear of abandonment from that day forward because that's how my father's death left me feeling. I don't remember telling anyone, not even my mother, that I felt abandoned.

The family secret prevented me from saying goodbye to my father. I have been told that children didn't customarily attend funerals in Australia at that time. While the funeral was on, my sister and I went to stay with a kind neighbour. We did, however attend the wake at our home. I honestly don't remember anything about it, but I can imagine that the atmosphere would have been pretty sombre.

Knowing how Dad had really died helped me understand the cruel behaviour of his mother and brother towards my sister and me. Earlier in the book, I described how their behaviour was changing before his death and continued afterwards. They acted as if it was our fault their son and brother had died, which, of course, it wasn't. The stigma of suicide was partly to blame for their behaviour. For me, their behaviour was another abandonment.

In 2011, when I finally learnt the truth about my father's death, I tried to find out as much information as possible. There was an urge to fill in the knowledge gaps. My first stop was the hospital where he died. I was unsuccessful in my attempt to obtain his medical records. The hospital records clerk told me that they had been destroyed. Maybe true, maybe not. While I was disappointed, I didn't pursue it further. I didn't feel sufficiently drawn to delve further into the mystery.

In 2023, I believe there is probably information pertaining to my father's death. For example, a Coroner's report would have been prepared, as well as a police report. I know that it was a police matter because they had notified Mum of the death. At the time of writing this book, I'm not sure if I will put effort and energy into obtaining that information. It's the past, and it won't bring my father back. Besides, I have other goals to pursue, such as my new education business.

I still think about Dad, and his picture is on my bookcase. The picture was taken at the property in the South West of WA, and he is smiling. I think he felt like he'd taken a small step towards his dream of being a farmer, although he wasn't going to work on the land full-time. It was destined to be a citrus orchard, not a cattle farm.

Chapter 9
Endings and New Beginnings

Endings and new beginnings are intertwined; you can't have one without the other. Years ago, I read an inspiring story called *Tuesdays with Morrie.*[9] The author, Mitch Albom, shares the wisdom he received during his regular visits with Morrie, who was terminally ill. The lessons Mitch learned from Morrie changed his life for the better, and enriched it. While Morrie's life was ending, it was the beginning of Mitch's life as a mainstream author and novelist. He observes, 'All endings are also beginning. We just don't know it at the time.'[10]

Some of the endings in my life have been my choice. I chose to leave my teaching job with the WA Education Department in 1987. That was an easy decision. One day, at work, I realised I wasn't satisfied with my job. In the first week of term, fresh after a two-week holiday, I asked myself, 'Is this all there is?'

---

[9] Mitch Albom, *Tuesdays With Morrie*, Hachette Australia Publisher, 1998

[10] Mitch Albom, *The Five People You Meet In Heaven,* Little Brown Book Group, London, 2003

Endings and New Beginnings

My family were rather shocked, to say the least, when I announced that I had found a new job and was leaving a secure government teaching position. I can't blame them; it all happened very quickly. A colleague told me about a job advertisement she'd seen for ESL teachers. At that time, in the late 1980s, Australia was entering the overseas student market, and private English schools were opening across the country.

During the short period of time I worked at the language school, I was given a leadership position. As the Deputy Principal, I had the opportunity to attend an international English teaching conference in Singapore.

I learned a lot from that position, including how to deal with a disorganised boss who had poor communication skills. For example, on one occasion, he neglected to tell me about an ad he'd placed in the main Perth newspaper, the *West Australian*, with my name as the contact person. Unfortunately, I hadn't seen the ad on the weekend, so I wasn't prepared for the barrage of calls on Monday morning. To this day, I'm not sure if he did it on purpose or was just hopelessly disorganised. Either way, I was furious at being put in that position without the information I needed.

Although the position was short-lived, I have no regrets about taking it. It was exciting to change direction in my career. I would wake up in the morning with a spring in my step, keen to go to work. It is said, 'A change is as good as a holiday', and that job was, at least in the beginning. By taking a leap of faith, and leaving a secure government job, I showed myself that I had the courage to go for what I wanted in life.

The end of my marriage after 22 years was a milestone event in my life. If I had known then what I know now, I wouldn't have stayed under the same room as my ex-husband for over a year! It wasn't healthy for either of us or our older daughter who was still at home. The atmosphere was so tense you could cut it with a knife.

After informing my husband that I wanted out of the marriage and that I no longer regarded myself as his wife, I began to act more assertively. For example, I stopped cooking, cleaning and washing for him. Those tasks were no longer in my job description. That was liberating for me because I no longer had the 'wife' role. I also stopped sharing a bed and moved into the bedroom at the other end of the house, vacated by our younger daughter when she moved to Melbourne. At least I didn't have to put up with his snoring.

While I was able to make these small but significant changes in the relationship dynamic, I wasn't able to start my new life as a single woman. I didn't even think about living by myself again until the home was sold in early 2013. The realisation about how much of myself I had relinquished during the relationship didn't hit me until I was living by myself. It had been a gradual process, and I had just adjusted to each surrender. After all, it made life easier in the short term, and I was trained to capitulate in my teenage years.

While studying with Bob Proctor, I learnt about the *Vacuum Law of Prosperity*.[11] This universal law states that you have to create space for what you want in life. For example, if you want a new car, you have to get rid of the one you already have. Bob used to say that nature hates a vacuum and will fill the space created as soon as possible. In the same way, I could never have met my current partner if I hadn't created a space in my life for him.

Looking back, I can see that the end of the marriage and living by myself for five years, set the scene for the next big ending in my life. It took a lot of courage to leave a relationship that I had been in for 25 years. I could easily have talked myself out of ending it; after all, I had done that over the years. There was sadness, but it would have been even sadder to stay in an unfulfilling marriage where I was taken for granted. I wasn't seen, heard or appreciated.

To move interstate as a single woman in my fifties took guts; I acknowledge that. However, after all I had been through in my life, I didn't see myself as brave at the time. I had been taught to be strong. I prided myself on my mental strength and resilience. My mother had shown me what strength looked like after Dad died. She had to do everything by herself, and I believed that was what being an adult woman involved.

For the first year or two that I lived in Melbourne, I continued to play the strong, independent woman role.

---

[11] Bob Proctor, *You Were Born Rich*, Life Success Publications, 1997

I had to depend on myself, not my adult children or a life partner. When I met my current partner in early 2019, I slowly started to soften and let this man support me. I wasn't used to having a man who respected me, saw me, heard and appreciated me. It took a while to feel safe to express my feelings.

I had barely been living in Melbourne for two years when the COVID-19 pandemic reached Australia. All of a sudden, the way of life we knew in Melbourne stopped. Dead in its tracks, so to speak. Although there was a lot about life during lockdown that I didn't like, it wasn't all bad. No situation is completely, one hundred percent good or bad because we live in a relative world. We couldn't appreciate the good if there wasn't anything to compare it to. I used to tell my daughters at the beginning of a new school term, 'You wouldn't appreciate the holidays if you didn't have school.'

My partner and I were incredibly fortunate to move into a rental house two weeks before the first lockdown. That was the end of about six years of living by myself, and I was ready for the change. It was a new adventure for me, but not a solo one. I found it so easy to work with my new partner to achieve common goals. For once, I didn't have to make all the decisions, or organise everything.

We rented that house for about eighteen months before moving to an apartment on the edge of the CBD. We love our current home with all the amenities and public transport on our doorstep. The Queen Victoria markets are within easy walking distance, as is the city centre. It's what I had when I first came to Melbourne, a car-free, active lifestyle.

When I returned to Perth in October 2022 to celebrate my sister's sixtieth birthday, I could appreciate aspects of life that I had taken for granted when I lived there. I had something to compare Perth to, for the first time. I was looking at Perth through fresh eyes. The pace of life was slower, and more relaxed. There was less traffic and travelling was easier. The beautiful, wide blue skies and the strong aroma of the Indian Ocean brought back memories.

If someone asked me before I visited Perth for the first time in three years, 'Would you go back to live in Perth?' My immediate, heartfelt answer was an emphatic, 'No'. When I was leaving Perth at the end of that visit, I told my sister that the answer to that question was no longer black and white.

For the foreseeable future, I will be dividing my time between Melbourne and Perth. That seems to be a reasonable compromise, the best of both worlds. When I spend time back in Perth with my family and friends, I feel connected to my roots. You can take the girl out of WA, but you can't take WA out of the girl. After all, my formative years were spent there. Until I left, I had no idea of the strength and depth of those roots.

Now that I have been living in Melbourne for five years, I have had many new opportunities and met a lot of new people. Some of them have become friends. I have made a new life for myself. I won't pretend that it was always a smooth process; moving interstate in my late 50s certainly presented challenges.

What I do know, without a doubt, is that my life in Perth had to end for the new me to emerge. The personal growth I have undertaken, and the awareness I have gained delights me. The book you are reading would never have been written if I hadn't embarked on my adventure. Most importantly, I would never have met my partner.

Chapter 10

Becoming Me

What does it mean to 'become' me? Wasn't I always me?

It means growing in awareness, on a conscious level, of my beliefs, habits, and attitudes. In other words, becoming aware of my previously subconscious paradigm. It involves examining and reflecting on established behaviour patterns and the way I move through life.

Through studying with Bob Proctor, I became aware, for the first time in my life, that I wasn't living wide awake. I was operating with a rule book that other people had written. My parents, grandparents and society in general, had passed down the rules, and I had just swallowed them. As a young child, up until the age of about seven, that was all I could do. However, by the time I reached adulthood, the rules had been thoroughly internalised, and I didn't question them.

The move from Perth was the catalyst for my awakening. The act of physically putting myself in a new place, a bigger city, opened the door to awareness.

While living in Perth, I had never heard of Bob Proctor or known anyone who was studying his material. Maybe I never would have discovered it if I hadn't come to Melbourne.

Bob Proctor woke me up in 2018. Over the course of the year-long program, I was repeatedly exposed to the notion of paradigms, how to change them, and how to overwrite the existing paradigm in my subconscious mind. I had never heard the term paradigm, which describes all our beliefs and habits. Realising that I have been conditioned by my family and society to think and behave like everyone else was life-changing.

I made a decision to start living by my own rule book, or as Bob Proctor often said, become the director of my own movie as well as the leading lady. What a liberating, empowering and daunting decision. I say daunting because, as the scriptwriter, leading lady and director of my own movie, I had to take full responsibility for my own results. There was no one else to blame if I didn't achieve my goals.

Through much introspection, I saw what wasn't working and needed to change. For example, I used to be an expert people-pleaser and went to great lengths to keep the peace in my marriage. While I understand where that habit originated, it wasn't something I wanted to continue. Gradually, I have replaced people-pleasing with assertiveness. A habit of a lifetime takes effort to extinguish, but it is definitely possible.

I credit my study with Bob Proctor with giving me the knowledge and skills to change my life. Naively, I thought that having achieved my goal of moving to Melbourne, I could do anything. However, I didn't know what I didn't know about living an authentic life. I had a lot to learn, and the learning curve was steep.

As with any learning, the process was neither linear or smooth. Early in the process, full of optimism and enthusiasm, I started to experience moderate levels of anxiety. I was confused because I thought I was moving in the right direction with my goal set and studying inspiring material.

At that point, I didn't understand that my subconscious mind was holding me back. It didn't want me to change; it was threatened by the new ideas I was encountering. So it used whatever techniques had worked in the past to keep me stuck. That's its job.

I learnt about the concept of the terror barrier, the metaphorical barrier that must be crossed in order to grow. The subconscious mind gets freaked out by the prospect of change and tries to scare you into abandoning the whole idea. To grow, to change your life, you have to push through the terror barrier, tell it that you're doing the new thing anyway.

Towards the end of 2018, I hit 'rock bottom'. After all the preparation for the move to Melbourne, the move itself, and setting up my new life, I was burnt out. However, as I had for many years, I just kept going. Resting wasn't an option. I had to find work and earn an income.

Since beginning my training with Bob Proctor, my paradigm has undergone a major change. Growing up, I believed an adult woman had to do everything by herself. She was the one who juggled parenthood, unpaid housework, paid work and caring for ageing parents. Regardless of whether a man was present in the household or not, that was an adult woman's role.

When I was married, I was unaware that I had a subconscious belief that I had to do everything by myself and that I wouldn't be supported by my husband. It was part of my paradigm and buried deep inside my subconscious mind. So, that is what I experienced in my life; I got what I believed. My experience mirrored my internal beliefs.

My new paradigm is a world away from the old model. For example, I no longer rush from one activity to the next like a 'headless chook'. Several times in my adult life, I have suffered burnout, which was not a pleasant experience. After the last burnout, I determined I would never go through it again. It was too painful, and it took months to recover. I made a conscious decision to live life at a slower pace and not overload myself.

Bob Proctor made a big impact on my life, without a doubt. I would not be where I am today without his materials, which I still study. There have been two other crucial influences on my personal growth journey. They are my partner and the COVID 19 pandemic.

My new paradigm of an adult woman includes a supportive partner who is also a friend. Unlike my mother, who didn't remarry after my father died, I have been fortunate to meet a wonderful man who sees, hears and appreciates me. Fortunate, but it wasn't an accident. I believe he sees me because I now see myself more fully. My self-esteem is the highest it has ever been, and I'm very comfortable in my own skin.

When we met, I was a very serious person. I'm pleased to say that over the five years we've been together, I've learnt to laugh; a lot. We have our own 'in jokes'. I have become playful and childlike again. That is such a gift he has given me, and I didn't even know I was looking for it.

Over the course of our relationship, I have also become assertive. Unlike when I was married, I have the freedom to change my mind, state my preferences and disagree with his opinion. My partner asks for my opinion and respects it. In my marriage, I used to be reluctant to express my opinion because it was sometimes ridiculed or dismissed. For example, one time, I remember my husband slamming his hand down on the table as he declared, 'your opinion is wrong'. I can't remember what I was wrong about.

I can grow in this relationship. My partner isn't threatened by my growth and encourages me to pursue my goals. For example, if I'm busy working on my business, he will cook the dinner. That means the world to me because I never had that level of support in my marriage.

In 2020, when the COVID19 pandemic reached Australia, my partner and I had just rented a house together. After two weeks in our new place, life as we knew it stopped. No-one could have predicted the craziness of those early weeks and months. I'm very glad that I didn't have to go through it alone, not being able to visit anyone or go anywhere.

As I learnt from Bob Proctor, there are only two ways to change a paradigm. One is an emotional impact. The COVID pandemic had an emotional impact on everyone who went through it. It changed us forever. It shocked us into realising that life as we knew it, could change very quickly. For example, during lockdown we couldn't go and have a hair cut. Something as routine as a hair cut was a risk to our health.

I'm definitely not the same person I was pre-COVID. For a start, I no longer take life for granted. For example, I write daily in my gratitude journal about how grateful I am to be alive and for the opportunities the day brings. It's a constant reminder to live fully today because that's all I have. Tomorrow is not guaranteed.

Actually, nothing is guaranteed in life. The lockdowns Melbournians endured meant that people's ability to earn an income was threatened. Like many people of my generation who had been raised to exchange time for money and work for an employer, I only had one source of income at the onset of the pandemic. I had heard about the concept of multiple sources of income from Bob Proctor, but it hadn't impacted me emotionally. Therefore, I hadn't done anything about it.

Wealthy people throughout history have always had many sources of income. If one failed, they could fall back on one of the others. That certainly wasn't what I learnt growing up. In fact, I had no financial literacy education and no idea about wealth creation. I changed my mind about wealth creation during the pandemic and determined to create alternative sources of income for myself. I never want to be denied a way of earning money because of an external event beyond my control.

During the COVID lockdowns, I had time on my hands. I was stuck at home by myself. Fortunately, I had the opportunity to write a short story for an anthology. I had never written anything for publication up until then. For some reason, I was attracted to the idea of contributing to the book, and I knew what I would write about; my move to Melbourne.

The story wanted to be written. It was like it had a life of its own. I can remember getting up at 2 am and writing the first draft in a couple of hours. The words just flowed from my memory onto the paper as I relived the experience. Writing that story and seeing it published began a new chapter in my life. I'm now a writer. It's part of my self-image.

I confess; I have the writing bug. I've fallen in love with writing. Writing this book has not only helped me hone my craft, it has enabled me to gain insights that I never got through talking to counsellors or psychologists. Maybe I access a different part of my brain when I write. Some chapters have been harder to write about; my marriage for example. Sometimes, after writing about a particularly painful experience, I had to put it aside and process what I had written.

My personal growth journey will continue for the rest of my life. Just like my grandfather, who took up oil painting in his eighties, I have become a writer in my sixties. It's never too late to learn something new. In the next chapter, I share what I have learnt about a system for personal development called Human Design. It's the newest tool I have found to understand your uniqueness as a human being.

Chapter 11
A Life-Long Learner

Growing up, the importance of education and learning were impressed on me by my parents, particularly my mother. She often said, 'Education is something that can never be taken away from you.' Consequently, my sister and I were expected to finish all 12 years of formal schooling and undertake post-secondary education. Our horizons were broadened by overseas travel and we read widely as well.

In the 1960s and 70s when I was at school, education was synonymous with information gathering. If I could take in the information, successfully regurgitate it in an essay or exam, I thought I knew it. No; I knew *about* it. There's a big difference between knowing *about* something and knowing it. Knowing something, as I've come to understand through studying personal development, means my behaviour is different as a result. For example, knowing about the benefits of exercise isn't the same as making daily exercise a habit in my life.

The focus of formal education was on the content to be learnt, not the learning process. I knew how to memorise, but not think. I could not have named the

A Life-Long Learner

six mental faculties that humans have in place of instinct, let alone use them. They are imagination, intuition, reason, will, memory and will. Unfortunately, this is still the case in many educational institutions in Australia, according to what I have heard from school students I've coached.

Alvin Toffler, the author of *Future Shock*[12] wrote back in 1970, 'The illiterate of the 21st century will not be those who cannot read and write, but those who cannot learn, unlearn and relearn.' In my opinion, that makes a commitment to life-long learning a necessity for success in the modern world. Not just in relation to the outside world, but also learning about our inner world. In other words, understanding who we really are and what makes us tick.

My personal growth journey will continue as long as I'm alive. That's a commitment I've made to myself. In late 2023, I discovered the Human Design System[13] which has further added to my understanding of my uniqueness as a human being. It is a complex, multi-layered system which combines Western Astrology, Chinese I Ching, Hindu Chakra system and quantum physics amongst others.

Although I am in the early stages of my learning journey, I'm fascinated by what Human Design has already shown me. The first step was obtaining my chart, based on my birth date, time and place. There

---

[12] Alvin Toffler. *Future Shock*, Random House New York, 1990.

[13] Created by Ra Uru Hu, and published in a 1992 book, *The Human Design System*.

are internet sites which provide Human Design charts free of charge, such as https://mybodygraph.com and https://jovianarchive.com/Get-Your-Chart.

Once I had my chart, I started studying how to read it. One book that I found very interesting and useful was *Human Design: How to Discover The Real You* by Chetan Parkyn. I also undertook a foundational, self-study online course for my aura type, Projector, presented by The Projector Movement. Their website is: https://www.theprojectormovement.com.

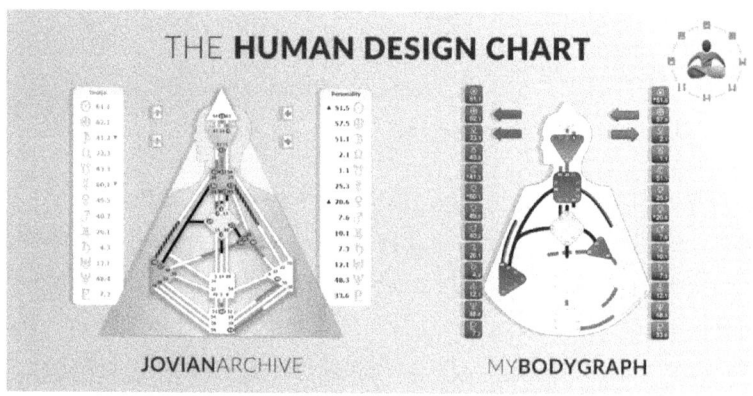

Image https://jovianarchive.com

Looking at this chart, the two diagrams show the body's energetic system, the nine energy centres and the channels through which energy flows between them. It also shows the 64 gates of the Chinese I Ching system. Some of the centres are coloured, or defined, and are consistent throughout life. These represent the true self. The white centres are referred to as undefined and show where a person is likely to be conditioned, or shaped, by the outside world.

On either side of the diagrams are two columns of numbers and symbols, one in black, one in red. The black numbers represent the positions of the sun, moon, and planets at the time of birth and describe aspects of a person's personality. The person will be consciously aware of these characteristics. On the other side, the red column of symbols and numbers represent the position of the sun, moon, and planets approximately 88 days before birth. This is referred to as your design date. These numbers represent the nature of your body intelligence of which a person isn't consciously aware.

The first and most important aspect of the Human Design is the energy type. In this way it is similar to Carol Tuttle's Energy Profiling system. There are four aura types, Generator (including a subtype, Manifesting Generator), Manifestor, Projector and Reflector. Some authors talk about Manifesting Generator as a distinct type. My type is Projector and about 20 percent of the world's population are this type.

Since discovering that I have the Projector energy Type and researching my chart, I can clearly see that I have not lived my true nature. That's not really surprising, as Human Design originated in the late 1980's. By then, I had lived nearly 30 years of my life with no idea of my energy type. However, now that I have the information, I can start to live according to my true nature.

Another basic aspect of Human Design is strategy. Each type has a Strategy for using energy in interacting with other. As a Projector, my strategy is to wait to be invited to share my wisdom, insights and advice. In the meantime, while waiting for the invitation, I am meant to play, study, and hone my skills. I was excited to learn that I was meant to play and have fun, because for most of my life I was a very serious person. In the past, I would have told everyone I met about Human Design and encouraged them to get their chart. The information would have fallen on some deaf ears and would have been a waste of my energy. Now, I only introduce it to people who are open to learning more about themselves.

Authority is another basic component of Human Design. This is the way a person is designed to make decisions. For example, my Authority is intuitive, so I'm supposed to listen to the subtle 'voice' of my intuition. That is something I have been familiar with for quite a long time, and I can clearly recall situations in which I have used it. I'm not the sort of person who's meant to spend a long time making decisions.

The Awareness variable refers to how we learn, assimilate, and recall information and knowledge. If the arrow faces right, the person has Receptive Awareness and takes a big-picture approach to learning. If the arrow faces left on the other hand, the person has Strategic Awareness and takes a more detailed approach to learning. As an educator, this is valuable information to be able to share with students.

The other piece of information that relates to learning is the Profile. Everyone has one of the twelve profiles, which is comprised of two numbers. For example, mine is 4/1, the Opportunist/Investigator. This is a useful website describing the profiles: https://humandesign.zone/profile

Bob Proctor wrote and taught extensively about making decisions, a necessary skill for success in life. He stated that making a decision immediately raises a person's vibrational level and moves the body into action. Since studying Bob's materials, I am better at making decisions. Understanding how I was designed to make decisions gives me extra confidence in the process.

There are numerous books, courses and YouTube videos about Human Design if you feel inspired to delve into this system. I don't claim to be an expert; just sharing some of what I've learnt. I believe that my introduction to Human Design was perfectly timed for me. Unlike when I discovered Bob Proctor's materials, I didn't believe I should have known it earlier in my life. It probably wouldn't have made sense when I was younger. Besides, now I have the time to really research it to my heart's content.

Author Bio

Heather Thorne

Heather was born and raised in Perth, Western Australia. The older of two daughters, she came from a small, tight-knit family. Growing up in the 1960's, parents were firmly in-charge, and life was orderly. Heather's childhood ended abruptly with the death of her father in 1971.

Heather undertook teacher training after finishing school and has been an educator in a variety of settings. In 2022, she established her own education business, HT Education. Its mission is to change the paradigm of adult English as a Second Language (ESL) instruction in Australia and offer an alternative to traditional classroom learning.

In 2018, Heather packed up her life in Western Australia and moved to Melbourne. It was a life-changing decision in ways that she couldn't have foreseen at the time. She was looking for adventure, to live life on a bigger stage, and she has achieved that goal.

Heather is a proud mother of two adult daughters who are highly accomplished and independent young women who also live in Melbourne. She happily shares her life with her partner of four years, who has shown her how to laugh and relax.

Appendix

Information on Energy Profiling by Carol Tuttle

I discovered Energy Profiling in 2013, soon after my marriage broke up, and I was living by myself for the first time in 25 years. During my marriage, I had given up a lot of myself without realising it. So, it was a time of personal *recovery*, picking up the missing pieces.

Prior to learning about Energy Profiling, I was unaware that energy flows through our bodies on a continual basis. We just can't feel it happening. Carol Tuttle, a healer, and Energy Psychologist developed a system of categorising people according to the way in which energy flows through them. The system consists of four Types, Type 1, Type 2, Type 3, and Type 4.

Tuttle maintains that everyone has a mixture of all four Types, but one will be dominant. She has developed a short, fun quiz to help people determine their Type. However, the most accurate way to determine your Type is by examining facial features together and separately. For example, I was fascinated to learn that the shape of my eyes, eyebrows, nose, and the texture of my skin all reflected my Type 3 energy.

As well as a dominant Type, everyone will have a strong secondary Type. Mine is Type 2, for example. I was particularly interested to learn that children often over-develop their secondary energy Type if they are shamed for being their natural selves. As a child, I remember being told to be quieter and calmer. So, I became softer, gentler like a Type 2. Through no fault of their own, my parents had no idea of my energy Type. Sometimes, my energy was too dynamic and fast for them to handle, I guess.

People who lead with Type 1 are the ones who light up the energy in a room when they enter it. They love to have fun. It's their primary motivation for doing anything. As adults, they may have a high-pitched, childlike voice and be exuberant in their movements. For example, they may think nothing of wearing a dress-up costume even when there's no party to go to and skip around squirting people with a water pistol in the shape of a flower.

Type 1s are the ideas people, and they believe anything is possible. In a work situation, they may say, 'We can do this,' and their enthusiasm is infectious. In one company I worked for, one of the senior managers was a Type 1. He was great at coming up with ideas, but it was left to others to bring them to fruition.

People who lead with Type 2 energy are motivated by comfort. The furniture they sit on has to be comfortable, the clothes on their body, and the water temperature has to be just right. One of my daughters is a Type 2 and prefers to buy second-hand clothes for this reason. Someone else has worn them in, so to speak.

For Type 2s, emotional comfort is also important in interpersonal relationships. For example, they hesitate to say something which may hurt someone's feelings. That's because Type 2s are the reserved, gentle, sensitive people in the Energy Profiling system. They move through the world smoothly and quietly. When they walk, they seem to glide along the floor or pavement.

Type 3s described by Carol Tuttle as rich and dynamic. They move swiftly into action and are motivated by results. For example, as a Type 3, I have always enjoyed jobs like ironing because I could see when I had reached the bottom of the ironing basket. So often, in my teaching career, it would take a while to see the results of my efforts. Type 3s walk in a determined way, with a heavy foot fall. My mother used to say that she could always tell it was me coming up the front stairs by the way I walked.

In the workplace, Type 3s put the plan that Type 2s created into action. In my last job, I would be frustrated by other people's slowness to act. I would have my sleeves rolled up and be raring to go. When I put on a long-sleeved top or cardigan, I immediately push up the sleeves to mid-forearm. Even in cold weather, I never wear sleeves down to my wrists. Results were what motivated me; the completed report, the stage of a project completed.

Then there's Type 4s whose movement is the slowest of all the four Types. It is straightforward, succinct, and precise. In fact, you may hear a Type 4 say, 'exactly' or 'precisely' when agreeing with someone. Those aren't words I would use very often. Precision and perfection aren't so important to me as a Type 3. My sister is a Type 4 and is very particular about certain things, such as the way she presents food on a plate or decorates a table.

In a work situation, Type 4s are motivated to improve performance. They can see where changes need to be made to do the job better in the future. The way they communicate is efficient, and they are economical in the use of words. This may come across as bluntness, even rudeness, but it's not their intention.

Carol Tuttle has applied Energy Profiling to clothing in a program called *Dressing Your Truth*. When I discovered how to express my Type 3 energy through my clothes, I eliminated all black clothing from my wardrobe. The energy is too dense for me. My sister, on the other hand, looks great in black. Funnily enough, unlike me, she never wore black as a younger woman. Now, as an older woman, she is the one who wears black, not me. Using the Style Guide, I was able to choose the right colours, patterns, and styles, and I have felt confident in my clothes ever since.

Another course I did with Carol Tuttle was called the *30 Day Money Cure*. That course gave me insights into how I handled money and how to improve my relationship with it. As a result of the course, I became aware of previously unconscious spending habits and why I shopped very differently from my sister. My sister, a Type 4, has always been an amazing money manager and bargain finder. The course is still available through the Carol Tuttle Healing Center.

I highly recommend reading Carol Tuttle's book, *It's Just My Nature! A Guide to Knowing and Living Your True Nature*. It's available online and is the definitive guide to Energy Profiling. She also has a YouTube channel and website (https://my.liveyourtruth.com).

www.ingramcontent.com/pod-product-compliance
Lightning Source LLC
Chambersburg PA
CBHW062039290426
44109CB00026B/2675